THE KEY TO EVERYTHING

JACK HAYFORD

THE KEY TO EVERYTHING

CREATION
HOUSE
BOOKS ABOUT SPIRIT-LED LIVING
ORLANDO, FLORIDA

Creation House
Strang Communications Company
600 Rinehart Road
Lake Mary, FL 32746
1-800-283-8494

Unless otherwise noted, all Scripture quotations are from the
New King James Version of the Bible. Copyright © 1979, 1980,
1982 by Thomas Nelson Inc., publishers. Used by permission.

Hardback:
First printing, November 1993
Second printing, May 1994
Third printing, June 1994

Paperback:
First printing, May 1995

To Him who loved us and washed us
from our sins in His own blood,
and has
made us kings and priests
to His God and Father,
to Him
be glory and dominion
forever and ever.
Amen.

For by Him
all things were created
that are in heaven
and that are on earth,
visible and invisible...
All things were created through
Him and for Him. And He is before
all things, and in Him all things
consist.

Revelation 1:5-6
Colossians 1:16-17

ACKNOWLEDGMENTS

I T WOULD be ludicrous to write a book on giving and then fail to give recognition to the people who actually made the book possible.

I used to read words of thanks like these in books, and I thought, "How generous and humble." But that was before I ever "worked a book through" to publication.

Today I know that generosity and humility have nothing to do with it. It's simply the absolute truth that many people were invaluable to this project. Simple honesty with the matter brings me to my knees, in thanks to God for these people, and to the keyboard, so that I can write thanks to the people themselves.

Thank you, Becki. You're such a dear daughter. Mom and I couldn't be prouder of you for any reason I can imagine. You're a we're-happy-you're-ours kid ("kid" hardly being the term for a gracious woman in her thirties). You're a loving wife, whose support to Scott [Bauer] makes his giftedness all the more fruitful as he ministers beside me. You're a devoted mother (who not only raises good kids but trains famous grandchildren to live God's way). And you are also a very fine speaker/teacher/writer/editor (who causes me moments of wonder that you'll give so much time to help your dad do a book when you could be writing one of your own!).

Your patience and steadfast work in distilling the foundational material from sloppy notes I'd scrawled and from roughly typed transcripts of taped sermons — then organizing it all into something that had a chance of becoming a book — is the first reason this work exists. Your dad appreciates that, thanks you and loves you a lot!

Thank you, Janet and Debbie.

My personal aide, Janet Kemp, and Creation House's editor, Deborah Poulalion, are the two who "made it happen" in terms of producing the manuscript and the book itself. To two good and godly women who love God's work and people, and give themselves unselfishly, I'm indebted and grateful.

As ever and always, to Anna, my wife, goes my deepest love and thanks. My name is always on my books, the same way Hayford has always been the name of our children. But when it comes to the love, strength and "bearing with" which brings each book "into the world," it's the same way it was with having our kids: You're the one who makes it possible for me to experience the joy I do. And I'm so happy we end up sharing it together.

CONTENTS

IN CASE YOU
WANT TO...

I'M OFFERING a few thoughts about this book before you begin reading it.

I think you're going to like it.

First, because it's filled with stories. True ones. I think you'll laugh at some. Others will bring a smile — maybe one or two will prompt misty eyes. I hope so. I hope the whole spectrum of feeling happens as you read.

Second, because I haven't written with antiseptic isolation from life. I've written about tough times, dumb times and learning times in my life — times I didn't realize it, but I was being drawn toward finding life's most essential "key."

You can go ahead now and read. I start with one of the funniest (and one of the most stupid) moments of my life.

From there, I think you'll be able to move quickly and, I hope, enjoyably through this small book.

So skip what follows and go ahead, start the book.

Unless you're suspicious.

If you become as suspicious as I do when anything sounds too simple, you may want to read just a little more of this preface. If you've thought, "Can *anything* be the key to *everything?*" you might want to give me about three minutes extra — here, up front — to hear my thinking on the *simple* and the *simplistic*.

On the Simple and the Simplistic

An essential difference between God and man is that what God creates always reveals a beautiful simplicity, while what man creates becomes increasingly more complex.

This certainly isn't due to greater intelligence in the creature than the Creator. Most of us have learned and accepted that the complex is superior to the simple.

The *simple* should never be confused with the *simplistic*. *Simple* defines what is "free from vanity, unadorned, unmixed." *Simplistic* is "to reduce a matter to a false simplicity by ignoring other factors." *Simple* maintains an original order of innocence without confusion. *Simplistic* claims to do the same but overlooks or bypasses essential parts or elements.

On the subject of this book, it seems to me that too much has been said about "giving and God's blessing" that is *simplistic*; saying true things about God's *hand* of abundance but too few things about His *heart* on the subject. I hope this book might be a return to the simple, not as superficial but as rooted in what is *central, foundational* and *ultimately essential.*

Recent years have realized a great deal of written thought and verbal thunder about how to find health and wealth. Because of our basic poverty as a race, any proposal of a solution — any promise of discovering or recovering prosperity — starts a gold rush. Just as multitudes dashed frantically for California in 1849 or for Alaska in 1898, our human quest for sufficiency and security lures us to quick answers for our needs, whether material, emotional or spiritual.

To my view, most approaches to the subject of our having enough of what it takes to live are simplistic, no matter how detailed. I think it's because they separate the requirements of character from the pursuit of plenty. Even among Christians, the path to abundance is too often indicated by *formulas* rather than by *formation*; that is, by offering ways to wealth without calling the soul to change.

God does want each human being to have more than merely "enough"; our Creator is a loving Father who desires our abundance as well as adequacy, and our prosperity as well as sufficiency. But I don't believe He offers this possibility on demand or without our returning to the simple.

The *simple* fact is that God has created us and "given us all things richly to enjoy" (1 Tim. 6:17) but that He has *not* tied that enjoyment to riches. He has linked it to a greater reality.

In the following pages I do deal with certain principles of stewardship — that is, how we think about and manage our money. But I could never have titled this book *The Key to Everything* if "everything" only related to the realm of the material or financial. That would have been *simplistic.*

Instead, I am inviting you to join me in looking at the dynamic link between life's fountainhead and life's finances; between God's promise and power in *forgiveness* and His release of everything else in *life* — including material sufficiency — if we'll learn to live at that fountain.

I think it's *simply true.* And I hope it might become a point of *simple power* because it centers the Key to Everything in God's heart rather than merely in His hand.

Jack W. Hayford

The Church On The Way
Van Nuys, California
October 1993

ONE

EXCESS BAGGAGE

My bag had begun
to multiply into
baggage — a burden
to my soul
born of a bad attitude...
Such things take
a phenomenal toll.

TO SAY that the Key to Everything could be found on a jet airplane may strike you as rather superficial. But if an experience of mine could prove that — at least for me — this particular flight to Portland was it.

It was Sunday.

Sundays are more than simply busy when you pastor a congregation with four morning services, and that's the way it had been. The congregation had packed into the chapel, and every ninety minutes another service had started (an amazing logistical accomplishment since the services ran eighty to eighty-five minutes each!).

On top of that, I'd hurried to the Burbank airport after the fourth service, incredibly grateful that the group inviting me to speak that night in Portland had arranged a first-class ticket. That would allow more space for rest and give me a chance to take off my shoes and stretch out before having to speak again that night.

It was strategic in terms of time, too. Having a seat in the front of the aircraft would allow me to disembark quickly upon arrival and be able to meet my hosts immediately so they could "get me to the church on time" for the evening service. It was tight, but plans were in place — that is, until the episode I call "The Saga of the Cluttered Baggage Compartment" occurred.

Because I knew that I would be going directly from the plane to the church service, and since it was just an overnight trip, I was carrying only a garment bag. Nothing to check in or wait for upon arrival in Portland. I would just get off the plane with my bag, and I'd be on my way. From my many travels I knew that, for the convenience of the passengers sitting in first class, there was an area specifically set aside to hang their garment bags. And I knew it was *guarded* for that purpose, because in my many, many non-first-class flights I had, on an occasion or two, tried to hang my bag there. But I would be told, "No, sir. This is for first-class passengers only!"

However, now with my first-class ticket in hand, when I started to give my bag to the flight attendant for placement in "my" compartment, she smiled sweetly but then shrugged and gestured with embarrassment toward the compartment.

It was already jammed with garment bags!

As I glanced over her shoulder, noting that in first-class seating there were only two people, I suddenly realized I'd been betrayed. I frowned and said nothing but inwardly shouted my protest: "This woman has let *just anybody* hang garment bags in my first-class place!"

The discovery disturbed me, especially because I had often been disallowed use of that area when *I* didn't have a first-class ticket. Now why didn't the same rule apply to all of these other people?

The cogs in my mind were starting to spin at full speed: "This time I *do* have a first-class ticket. Now I don't have a place for my garment bag! I don't like this!" (I still didn't say anything, but I was "ticked big time," as it's said in the vernacular.)

Of course, the flight attendant was very accommodating about the situation. She expressed her regret, offered to put the bag in one of the rear compartments for me and smiled her most gentle apologies.

I had in no way verbalized or revealed my anger, carefully containing my frustration. So I smiled back, saying that I would really appreciate it. But as she took my bag and moved toward the rear of the plane to hang it up for me, I hardly felt like smiling on the inside.

I'm not really a crotchety kind of person. In fact, I think almost everyone from family to associates would say I'm easy to get along with. But at this moment? Well, I'd gotten up quite early, preached four services, run to catch a plane — and I was tired. And so getting on the plane and having this happen caught me at a low point. I was annoyed.

The situation was really getting under my skin, for as I took my seat, the problem magnified in my mind. My garment-bag space had been given away! Now when I got ready to leave the plane, I'd have to

- go to the back of the plane,

- struggle through the tide of exiting passengers,

- try to get my garment bag back down a crowded aisle and

- only hope to catch my ride in time.

Surely you're starting to sympathize with me. Hey! I mean, was this a monstrous miscarriage of justice or what? You know what I mean? And all because that flight attendant gave away *my* garment-bag space!

I twisted a time or two in my seat, repressing frustration and trying to keep my overt attitude reasonably "Christian," but my mind kept replaying that scene of neglect and failure — no place for my bag! I decided something needed to be done about this. (Has anything like this ever happened inside you?)

Now, I thought, I'm far too nice a person to complain to the cabin crew or speak meanly or make trouble. But this whole matter was bigger than my problem, as anyone could see. C'mon. Haven't you had such moments when you thought, "Any person can see that the scales of universal justice are about to tip irretrievably toward tolerated irresponsibility in the workplace?"

That's where I was that day, thinking, "It may just be my bag today, but who knows what'll happen next? Y'know?" Somebody needed to do something, and I was the man for the mission.

"I'm gonna write to the airline!" I vowed silently. "After all, if they don't know something's wrong, they can't do anything about it. And if they don't do anything about it, pretty soon, every time anyone got on an airplane, that little compartment would be full of non-first-class-passenger garment bags!" I needed to take this right to the top so systems could be firmed up, a policy statement issued or something legislated in Washington!

By now I had forgotten about my need for a nap. I had a heavy-duty project on line, so I got my notepad out of my briefcase to jot down a few notes regarding what I wanted to say — the flight number, airport, destination and so on.

But as I got ready to write, it suddenly occurred to me that I was presuming that the flight attendant had filled up the front compartment before the back was used. Maybe by some fluke of circumstance, the back compartment had been filled up, and she had been forced to use the first-class compartment. To make an honest claim, I needed to find out. I had to be sure that I had a case. (Don't you think it admirable of me to have been so considerate of that possibility? Clearly "godly" reasoning was operating!)

I started to get up from my seat, planning to go to the rear of the plane to check out the possibility, when it happened.

The Lord spoke to me.

He spoke to me by a whisper of the Holy Spirit. (It often happens when you're about to do something really dumb!)

The plane still hadn't taken off, and just as I rose, the Voice said, "Let it go." That's all He said: "Let it go."

I wish I could tell you that every time I've heard the voice of the Lord, I have responded immediately. But I haven't. Not that I rebelled, mind you. I just didn't respond — didn't acknowledge He'd spoken. And I didn't obey.

It wasn't exactly complete disobedience but more of a suspended-in-time, I'll-obey-later disobedience. I didn't have an aggressively defiant attitude, but rather a passively convenient, try-to-look-innocent-while-saying, "I didn't hear anything, did you?" sort of denial. I was pretending not to have been addressed correctively by the Almighty. So, taking advantage of my "convenient denial" and "suspended obedience," I got out of my seat and started down the aisle.

There's no way in the world I could have known.

About two-thirds of the way to the back of the plane, sitting in the aisle seat, was a little four-year-old boy. I didn't see him, and so I didn't know that this particular four-year-old boy had just finished drawing a picture with a felt-tip pen and now was leaning over to show his mother what he had drawn. Nor did I see that as he stretched out his left hand, which was holding the picture to show his mom, his right hand, in symmetrical action, stretched into the aisle — holding the uncapped felt-tip pen.

It was absolutely perfect timing. Just as I arrived at his row on my "mission," a four-year-old arm appeared, pen in hand, and I was painted with a streak of black felt-tip ink right across the front of my very light-colored slacks!

Do you get the picture? I was going back to gather information to write a letter to the president of the airline when the God of the universe took the hand of a four-year-old boy and wrote a letter to me: "Let it go!"

You would think that at this point I would have recognized the fact that God was serious about my letting it go and that I would have become alert to my blinded-by-frustration attitude and gone back to my seat. But I had already "conveniently" ignored the voice, was wrestling a bad attitude and now had ruined the only pair of slacks I had brought with me. Still, instead of turning back, I thought, "Well, since I've gone this far, I might as well finish." (Talk about zeal for a cause!)

It was only about four steps later that I met one of the flight attendants who was trying to unlatch something on one of the soft-drink serving carts. Just as I got to her, something flipped loose, and a whole tray of soda cans came tumbling out onto the floor right in front of me. It was only because I have reasonable athletic agility that I managed to execute a leaping maneuver that kept me from tripping over the rolling cans — a marvel that I didn't break something. But now I was starting to think thoughts like: "There's a Jonah on board this plane — me!" Message number three came through: "Go sit down!"

Now, I ask you, what would you have done at this point, knowing you had only six feet more to go and you'd be at the rear luggage rack? You guessed it. I forged ahead, propelled by one thought: I've gotta know! Is the back compartment full, or did that flight attendant insensitively and irresponsibly give away my space?

The tenacity of a mind that is set on righting the wrongs of the world is an amazing barricade against good sense. So I took those last two steps and arrived at my goal. I confirmed what I'd hoped for: It was empty!

Aha! So I was right.

There were no garment bags hanging back there except mine and one other. Therefore, that flight attendant had indeed given away my garment-bag space to people who should have had theirs back here!

With this, the fruit of my investigation in hand, I was ready to write my letter, confident in the justice of my case. But something inside was changing. As I turned around and started back up the aisle, I knew my "find" was an empty victory. Actually, when the cans of soda were rolling around my feet, I'd begun to realize it was all over. My stupidity was being signalled with flashing lights, and I was finally ready to admit it. I had lost my cause.

So now, as I carefully stepped through the scattered cans of soda, edged my way around where the little boy was sitting and walked back down the aisle, I knew the letter wouldn't be written. I'd walked all the way to the back of the plane, trying to pump life into a mission that was on a dead-end street.

I was tired.

My "grudge" load had become too heavy. I had started with a complaint against the flight attendant, built it to air-line-president proportions, compounded it by dulling my ear to the voice of the Lord, paid for it with a pair of ruined slacks and punctuated it all with a waltz through a fleet of flying cans of soda.

It was enough.

My *bag* had begun to multiply into *baggage* — a burden to my soul born of a bad attitude about a mere garment bag. (Sometimes we humans can carry a grudge for a week or a month — or not even recognize that we have one in our back pockets from a years-ago incident. Such things take a phenomenal toll.)

I knew I needed to unload. I needed to settle things right then and there and get rid of my excess baggage.

Even before I got back to my seat, I had started apologizing to God. I knew I didn't have anywhere else to go, anyone else to address or any letters to write. I knew that I'd been corrected by the Head Corrector. My trip to the rear of the plane had been an exercise in the futility of fleshly efforts at self-justification and petty vindication, and a felt-tip marker streak on my slacks was setting in as a permanent memorandum of my pettiness.

I knew what I had to do: I needed to pray. I needed to confess my suddenly soured attitude and repent for my oh-too-human reaction.

When I sat back down, I closed my notepad. My smallness was over, and with a restored sanity now recovering the moment I prayed: "Lord, forgive me for once more becoming so prepossessed with the notion that it's my burden to 'balance the scales of universal justice.' That's too big a job for me to handle. Only Your hands can do that."

I could feel muscles in my body relax as I continued, "And, Jesus, forgive me for my pitiful smallness of soul — for stumbling into this trap of self-righteous stupidness."

I paused in my prayer, pensive and introspective. I wasn't done; I knew it. The Spirit was flushing out corners of corruption which had so quickly been spilled over my soul — even by so small an incident. I clearly felt I needed to pray even further, for I recognized my tainted attitude didn't end with my disturbance toward the general situation. There were specifics to deal with. First, my angered attitude toward the flight attendant. (I hadn't shown it, but it had somehow nested inside.) Then, the puniness of my soul that leaped at blaming the whole airline. (I confessed my sickening need to register blame.)

But I still wasn't finished. I continued to pray. "Lord, I do forgive that flight attendant for whatever oversight she made that inconvenienced me. I can't imagine, Lord, how many times my oversights and failures may have 'inconvenienced' Your purposes or those of other people."

How often have we sought to unload our frustration by registering blame or becoming angry, even when there wasn't a logical basis for our case? How could I be so blind as to say that the flight attendant slipped up, without remembering my own record of a lifetime of unintended "slipups"?

I've learned the wisdom of "praying all the way out" anything unworthy that seeks to lodge inside my heart, rather than leaving even the smallest foothold for the adversary to play on later. I continued to wait on the Spirit's quiet dealings with me as I sat there, prayerful but looking out the window at the sun-filled sky. There was still one more thing to attend to.

There seemed to be no real reasoning to support a yet-lurking irritation I discovered under the Holy Spirit's searchlight. But as I continued praying, I knew one more party needed to be "forgiven." I say "forgiven," not because the person was truly guilty of any conscious failure on his part, but because an accidental action had affected me, and I needed to "let go" — to release *him*.

It sounds so small that I hate to admit it. But I needed to "speak out" to God — to confess my feeling — about the little boy. I was irked about getting my pants messed up with that marker. And while I knew there was no legitimate blame a real adult could register against a four-year-old, I still needed to untangle the web of internalized irritation I'd allowed to be spun in my soul. I couldn't blame him — I *wouldn't* blame him. (In fact, if I had suspended my "suspended obedience," the streaked-slacks event never would have happened!) So I prayed again, haltingly, feeling the ridiculous nature of my so-quickly accrued collection of attitudinal sins: "And, Lord, I forgive the little boy."

While all this was taking place, things were starting to loosen up inside me — internal stress which had tensed more of my being than I'd noticed until that moment. But as I prayed, I could consciously feel my forearms release and relax. How quickly, without my notice, they had become taut! Yet now, my prayers of repentance, confession and forgiveness were working a small miracle, for I could feel myself coming unwound in the right way. I had finally let it go.

The plane took off, and I went to sleep. When we landed, I made it on time to the church, and — can you believe it? —

something wonderful happened. That night there was a remarkably precious and powerful move of the Holy Spirit in that meeting! When the service was over, as I was rejoicing in the beautiful visitation of God we had experienced, I was humbled before Him. I thanked Him profusely for helping me keep from "binding up" the potential of that evening, for I knew its loveliness never would have happened if I hadn't let go of what had occurred on the plane.

You're right: It would have been best if I'd let go sooner. But, thank God, I did surrender it before it was too late for that night's gift of His grace — a gift I don't believe His hand could have released had I not given up my handfuls of ungraciousness.

The Key to Everything — to releasing me from smallness, my soul from bitterness and for that evening blessing — was in giving. In this case, giving up and letting go — in *forgiving*.

It's a key that turns a lot of directions, but all of them turn "loose."

TWO

IDENTIFYING
THE KEY

*Learning and applying
the Key to Everything
involves the growing
of a heart attitude
in giving, which gives
the right thing
at the right time
in the right way and
for the right reasons.*

S UPPOSE MY garment-bag episode was cast in the form of an ancient parable. Suppose the "everything" truth — the key to releasing life — was put into Bible-sounding words. What if Jesus told my story to point out my petty, quick-to-anger, ready-to-blame, sudden-to-set-it-right-my-way episode? Might it sound like this?

> The kingdom of heaven is like a man en route by jet to Portland, who was inconvenienced by an unintended oversight on the part of a flight attendant. But this man, who had been forgiven of all his sins by the love and grace of God, took it upon himself to exact his pound of flesh from a person who

didn't even mean to do anything wrong toward him. As a result, he got a stripe on the front of his pants and could have broken his leg, tripping over falling objects at a place he never should have been (Moreover, it was by reason of the Father's mercy he didn't fall over the soda cans and not because of the man's imagined athletic agility. For, yea, the man was out of condition and not nearly as quick-footed or adept as he thought himself to be!)

The man wandered into the far country of the rear of the airplane where he thought he could find evidence to justify his self-centered forgetfulness that mercy is to multiply through the Father's children. But he, coming to his senses, did repent, saying, "Father, I am a dummy."

And because God had already forgiven the man for even dumber things than that — not to mention the damning things of human sinning — He, in grace, gladly received the honest confession. Whereupon the man was restful in his soul, readied for his responsibilities and released unto special blessings in the Father's power and purpose.

Maybe the above might strike you as something less than a beautiful, literary adaptation of Jesus' style, but "the garment-bag saga" touches the heart of so many issues and unveils so many human response patterns that I've often retold it at my own expense. There's no way I can tell it and come up looking anything more than painfully human at best and disgustingly petty at worst. But in that one brief episode are all the elements of what most *hinders* life and what most *liberates* it. In other words, within that story are pointers toward the Key to Everything.

Before you read any further in this book, let me tell you directly what that Key is: It's *giving*. To give is to exercise the

Key to Everything. But the Key isn't simply to give in an abstract way or with no motivating reason. Nor is the Key utilized by means of a secret formula of words or in magic actions of social magnanimity or through intellectual brilliance. Rather, learning and applying the Key to Everything involves the growing of a heart attitude in giving, which gives the right *thing* at the right *time* in the right *way* and for the right *reasons*.

Such giving takes many forms.

- There are times to give *up*, not in resignation or in abandonment to despair, but in a surrender of self-righteousness.

- There are times to *for*give, that is, to release what otherwise could be retained as a grudge, as anger, as pain or as internalized stress because of perceived or real injustices.

- There are times to give *over*, to place into the hands of the Creator-Judge of the universe matters which only His might or His justice can sufficiently handle.

- There are times to give *to*, providing with generosity in assisting the circumstance of another human being or group.

- There are times to give *in* through simple obedience because the only wise God has shown principles and patterns for giving as a discipline, intending by these to release us from a self-centered, survival mind-set or from our all-too-human self-protecting fear of want or poverty.

- There are times to give *wisely* because we understand reciprocal laws of God which promise a bountiful return if we give. And that return is His way of making possible our learning to give *over and over* again with increasing resources and joyfulness.

In short, the Key to Everything involves *giving* everything but never in the way we most fear. For our fears have taught us that to give *any*thing is to be left with less, and to give *every*thing is to be left with nothing. But this deep affliction — the tendency of the human soul to knot with spasms of clutching, cloying self-protectiveness — is a soul-sickness directly related to mankind's separation from God (more on this in chapter 8). Once a genuine rebirth of the human spirit occurs, the seeds of a possible restoration of full freedom are sown.

But growth takes time.

Biologically, nine months in the womb, plus at least a dozen years following birth, only *begin* the growth of a human being who can think and care for anyone other than himself. Similarly, in our spiritual beings, our new birth in Christ is only the starting place for growth in a life that can learn to live in the spirit of God's releasing grace. God's releasing grace is that grace in life which causes us to give as we have received, forgive as we have been forgiven and trustingly care for and serve others as we have been entrusted with resources, gifts, time and influence.

The Spirit of Releasing Grace

The words *the spirit of God's releasing grace* create the foundation of all giving. They draw their truth from the highest principle of all — that love gives. They are rooted in God's love, which is the foremost of all the attributes of His Person and personality. It is God's love that not only mandates *His* giving and forgiving because His nature can do no other, but it is His love which also mandates that those who are born into His family learn to do the same.

This principle is at the heart of one of Jesus' most revealing parables. It's a story-lesson with the highest billing and the most sobering warning. The billing? Jesus presents it as a "kingdom" parable, saying, "The kingdom of God is like this."

Don't miss the importance of a kingdom parable. These words mean far more than "Here's a churchy idea." Instead, the concept of the kingdom of God entails the whole spectrum of truth as to 1) how God rules, 2) how He has made life to function, and 3) how we can align with His intended order and find the joy of seeing our lives work as they're supposed to. So, because He's introducing a kingdom parable, we know the Lord is about to set us straight on something that is fundamental to functional, effective and successful living.

Then there's the sobering warning at the end of this parable.

It's a double exclamation mark of a point: "So shall my Father do," Jesus says. But rather than elaborate all that can mean right now, let's just read the parable. See if you recognize any parallel points between Jesus' story and my "saga." Mine turned to blessing and release for the sole reason that I had earlier learned a little about the meaning in Jesus' story. I say "a little" because of my slowness in response time on the plane, a time which would be improved somewhat today, though I am still trying to learn a lot more. Join me, would you?

Here's Jesus' story:

> Therefore the kingdom of heaven is like a certain king who wanted to settle accounts with his servants. And when he had begun to settle accounts, one was brought to him who owed him ten thousand talents. But as he was not able to pay, his master commanded that he be sold, with his wife and children and all that he had, and that payment be made. The servant therefore fell down before him, saying, "Master, have patience with me, and I

will pay you all." Then the master of that servant was moved with compassion, released him and forgave him the debt.

But that servant went out and found one of his fellow servants who owed him a hundred denarii; and he laid hands on him and took him by the throat, saying, "Pay me what you owe!" So his fellow servant fell down at his feet and begged him, saying, "Have patience with me, and I will pay you all." And he would not, but went and threw him into prison till he should pay the debt. So when his fellow servants saw what had been done, they were very grieved, and came and told their master all that had been done. Then his master, after he had called him, said to him, "You wicked servant! I forgave you all that debt because you begged me. Should you not also have had compassion on your fellow servant, just as I had pity on you?" And his master was angry, and delivered him to the torturers until he should pay all that was due to him.

So My heavenly Father also will do to you if each of you, from his heart, does not forgive his brother his trespasses (Matt. 18:23-35).

The Right Reasons

I earlier observed that our challenge as disciples of our Lord Jesus, who gave us this parable, is to learn to give the right things in the right way at the right time and for the right reasons. Jesus' teaching in this vivid story deals with all those "right" things. He is issuing a lesson in forgiveness which reveals the need for *forgiving* others, giving *up* selfish interest and giving *in* to God's greater wisdom. But undergirding the whole, at the crux of the story, is the reason for such a mandate to forgiveness being issued.

Begin with me by securing in our understanding "the right

reason" for our giving. This is essential because the Key to Everything isn't a wand waved as a magic exercise. Instead, it's an attitude worked into the human heart through understanding God's heart and methods. The pivot point in Jesus' whole teaching is one central moment: the confrontation between the forgiving master and the unforgiving servant. The lord of the servant drives the point home with understandable force of speech:

> You wicked servant! I forgave you all that debt because you begged me. Should you not also have had compassion on your fellow servant, just as I had pity on you? (Matt. 18:32-33).

Jesus' message is pungently pointed: Forgotten grace breeds unforgiving living.

His analogy isn't obscure. The picture of God's greatness of grace in forgiving each of us our sins through the cross of Jesus Christ is clearly in view in the master's release of his debt-ridden servant. This is the reason, the pivot point, the power base from which the Key to Everything springs. Jesus makes the gift of God's love and salvation the starting point for our learning about giving through any of the multiple ways we are to learn. Whether mercy or money, forgiveness or finance, we must first see, receive and understand *His* grace as the fountainhead of our lives and growth in the grace of giving. The foundational elements for those insights and that growth are in the parable I just recounted.

First, the context of Jesus' telling of this story is significant. Peter had just expressed what to him seemed to be a gracious offer: "Lord, should I forgive people seven times?" (see Matt. 18:21).

Don't make any mistake: Peter was stretching well past the common expectations for forgiveness in his day. The schools of thought present in the religion of his time proposed that even God didn't forgive anyone more than three times! This had been deduced from the preaching of the prophet Amos, in which the judgment of God is repeatedly announced upon nation after nation "for three transgressions...and for four" (see Amos 1 and 2). The conclusion some rabbis had drawn was that God forgives and excuses three times, but when a fourth violation occurs, judgment strikes. So when Peter asked, "Lord, should I forgive seven times?" it ought to be noted that he honestly thought he was being very, very generous.

However, Jesus' answer must have stunned him and those with him.

> I do not say to you, up to seven times, but up to seventy times seven (Matt. 18:22).

The men He was addressing were not fools. They recognized immediately that Jesus was pointing to an unthinkable pathway of unrelenting forgiveness. In the seventy times seven equation, He was saying, "Never stop forgiving!" He wasn't suggesting the creation of books with 490 tiny squares on each page into which check marks could be tabulated until a person could finally be condemned with divine approval. Instead, He was saying what love does — just as 1 Corinthians 13:5 says, "Love doesn't keep score!"

Then, to give the whole matter of steadfast, unending forgiveness a basis for operation, He told a story. The story is both a profoundly simple and a marvelously complete picture of the salvation God has offered each of us through the cross. It clearly illustrated these truths:

- We are all God's created, accountable servants.

- The debt is our sins, which are greater than we can repay.

- Our destiny is a complete and total loss by reason of our debt.

- Our cry for God's mercy, when uttered, will always find a compassionate response.

- His forgiveness is total and unconditional; our debt is cancelled through Christ's dying in our place.

- Having been forgiven completely, we are expected to live in the same posture toward others.

Thus, central to Jesus' call to live a life of giving and forgiving is the truth that our debt before God has been paid by Him — entirely and freely. And He has done all this for us notwithstanding our responsibility for our sins and our helplessness to pay for them.

Is a Pause Needed?

Perhaps we should pause a moment. Because, if for any reason, dear reader, you have never come to a personal moment of deciding your own response to God's offered gift of forgiveness, with its companion promise of eternal life through Jesus Christ, let me invite you to that moment here and now.

You are, even as I am, in need of forgiveness for sin. Though an unpopular word, sin describes our failures and compromises — our conscious or unrecognized violations of God's law, as well as our intentional or accidental compromises of personal integrity or morality. As with the servant in the story, we *are* in debt. We *are* responsible for our sins — known or unknown.

No amount of philosophizing about special or difficult situations or the relativity of one evil in comparison with another can excuse us from our own contribution to the welter of human failure that clouds our world. And further, like the servants in the story, we have an accounting to give. The Bible affords us clear information on this matter: We can deal accountably and responsibly with our sin now and receive God's forgiveness. Or we can dodge, make excuses or not deal with them now, and, continuing in this irresponsibility, receive God's ultimate judgment.

However, the most beautiful words in the world declares His promise of release, forgiveness and eternal life if we receive God's gift now:

> For God so loved the world that He gave His only begotten Son, that whoever believes in Him should not perish but have everlasting life.
> For God did not send His Son into the world to condemn the world, but that the world through Him might be saved (John 3:16-17).

To build a life on the *foundation* of God's forgiveness, we each need first to drink at His *fountain* of forgiveness. So if you've never made the personal choice — the decision to accept God's love-gift in Jesus Christ (that "moment of personal response" I mentioned above) — let me issue you a warm invitation to do so.

Since many readers will have already made their decision and begun in Christ, they may proceed. But if you need to follow through in this regard, allowing God's Holy Spirit to bring you to an assured place of peace with God and a relationship with Him in Christ, please turn to the appendix at the end of the book for guidance and help in prayer.

Resuming With Our Study

Having paused, then, to make the above inquiry, let's resume our study.

In this story-lesson Jesus shows us the majesty and totality of God's forgiveness. It is the substance which forms the foundation for all of life — life *now*, life *eternal* and life *to be lived* in the spirit of God's release! In order to establish this foundation for our lives it is crucial that we sense the dimension of need the servant in Jesus' parable faced. His problem was debt — analogous to human sin.

- *He was helpless.* He had no point of appeal to excuse himself from the fact of his indebtedness. It was real, and it was unpayable. His words, "Give me time," only point to the incredible way the flesh will quail and plead for its own potential power to answer. The debt, in contemporary funds, would be in the neighborhood of one hundred million, and the man is a common wage-earner on a day-laborer's salary.

- *He was hopeless.* Jesus isn't describing God in personal terms when He describes the response of the servant's master: "His master commanded that he be sold, with his wife and children and all that he had, and that payment be made" (Matt. 18:25). This argues neither for God's attitude toward us nor for the possibility that such a sale would have paid so great a debt. But it builds on the custom of the time: The debtor was sold into slavery for cash, and the same was done with the family, which was broken up and scattered among buyers of the slaves. The net gain from the sale was given to the one owed as a small recompense.

Again, the analogy is pointed. Our inability to save ourselves and the totality of our lostness without Christ is depicted by Paul: "That at that time you were without Christ, being aliens...having no hope and without God in this world" (Eph. 2:12).

This is more than mouthing a few theological platitudes. Gaining a hold on the Key to Everything requires our getting a full grip on the enormity of the dimensions of our necessity to forgive. To whatever degree we fail to see and remember the totality of our helplessness and hopelessness, we will be proportionally at risk. It's the same risk to which the servant in the story succumbed — forgetfulness. Forgetfulness feeds our inability to see ourselves in the need or failings of others.

The servant's actions seem unimaginable — at least until we contemplate our own foibles of unforgiveness. Listen to the words and watch the actions of the just-having-been-forgiven-a-fortune servant who had also just had his family spared slavery through his master's mercy:

> But that servant went out and found one of his fellow servants who owed him a hundred denarii; and he laid hands on him and took him by the throat, saying, "Pay me what you owe!" (Matt. 18:28).

The picture couldn't be more graphic — "by the throat"!

Something about the man's violence shakes our sensitivities as we look at the absolute insanity of the horrible forgetfulness manifest here. The inability of the forgiven servant to translate his blessing into similar grace causes us to want to rise in indignant defense. Everything carnal in us screams, "Pound the dude into the asphalt, and set the other guy free!" But the purpose of the text isn't to incite our anger at anyone other than ourselves, for however guiltless we may plead to be, we've all given place to the same practice. Yet, since we probably didn't actually grab someone by the throat and demand a handful of cash, we can miss seeing ourselves in this parable. But the same spirit of unforgiveness is present when:

- I criticize a neighbor.

- I judgmentally condemn a gross sinner.

- I feel vindictive against an enemy.

- I speak unkindly to a relative.

- I reject someone who doesn't meet my social tastes.

- I tolerate condescending attitudes toward people of different ethnicity.

- I attack fellow Christians for practices or positions different from mine.

- I mock any human being or carry hatred or anger concerning another person.

In short, virtually every clash in human relationships is due to some expression of an unwillingness to *give* — to *forgive* failure or to *give understanding* concerning differences.

The relative smallness of the debt owed by the second servant is another key part of Jesus' message.

In contrast to the unpayable millions constituting the first servant's debt, the second man owed one hundred denarii. A denarius was only a coin of rather small value, so one hundred of them have been computed to amount to anything from mere pocket change — perhaps forty dollars by rough estimate according to some tables — to a maximum of several days' wages, depending on the job. But using the highest possible figure, it would still come within the range of an amount which could soon be paid. The man only asked for time: "Have patience with me and I will pay you all" (v. 29).

You would think the first servant would have been shaken awake by those words. They were a precise echo of the request he had made to his master, but he had been asking for time to pay millions, not a paltry forty bucks! Now, when he receives a reasonable request from another for extra time to pay back an infinitely smaller debt, he is oblivious to his fellow servant's plea for patience. The first man didn't ask the master to forgive his debt, either.

There are two drastic differences in the way each appeal is handled:

- In the first, the master "had compassion, forgave him the debt and let him go." This was done in the face of an impossible amount, and then the requirement of payment was totally removed.

- In the second, the forgiven servant cast his fellow servant into the debtors' prison, disallowing opportunity even for a schedule of repayment which could easily have been fulfilled.

Again, the human parallels abound. How soon we all forget the greatness of grace which looked beyond our faults and, seeing our needs, totally forgave us. How easily we fall prey to hasty judgment. How slow we are to measure the relative failure of those who violate us against the backdrop of our violations against God. Our sin seems too small in comparison; our guilt, somehow, not as failing as those who fail us. Yet amid all this, Jesus calls *us* unto accountability — to an accounting for our ease in forgetting the dimensions of our deliverance.

"The kingdom of heaven is like this," He says to us today. And there's no way either you or I can escape the implications of our present responsibilities as "kingdom people." We can't hide behind a cheap proposal that this "forgiving way" isn't to be lived out until we arrive in heaven. Jesus has come to bring heaven's rule into our hearts now! The forgiven are called to be forgiving — to the same degree that we have been entirely, unconditionally and graciously forgiven!

But this only begins the lesson which identifies the Key to Everything. Let's look at what Jesus teaches in the conclusion of the parable.

THREE

THE "STINGER" IN THE STORY

Peace of heart,
mind, soul and body
can only be enjoyed
when God's forgiveness
is transmitted through us
as fully as it has been
given to us.

THERE'S A punchline to the parable of the unforgiving servant. But it tends to be overlooked in the wake of his awesome arrogance. His insensitivity screams from the narrative with such force that the detailed consequences, as well as Jesus' final dictum, tend to go unnoticed. But a *problem*, a *penalty* and a *pronouncement* conclude the story.

The Problem

First, the problem is that the second servant is still in prison when the story ends.

I suppose that most readers would assume what I did for

years: that when the master heard of the horrible ingratitude manifest in the first servant, he simply let the other servant out of prison. But one day I made a startling discovery.

The text doesn't say that.

Neither do the facts of business dealings in society. Debts between two parties can't be forgiven by a third party. They may be paid but not dismissed. The fact is that the existing debt was between the two servants, and, technically, the master had no authority over their interpersonal business matter.

This is important to notice not just because it's a curious point in the text. But because it does, in fact, illustrate the nature of our human relationships. It reflects the truth that each of us who has a relationship with God still has to give attention to relationships with one another.

It's a sad fact, even among Christians, that too many of us find it acceptable to *be forgiven* without *being forgiving*. How many of us are confident of a relationship with God through Christ and still somehow feel we can carry an account of debt against fellow servants of the Lord? It's also a revealed fact that God can't do and doesn't do anything about inter-believer stresses — that is, not against our will.

You see, dear one, our relationships with one another are not administrated by God. He only administrates our personal relationships with *Him*. And if another person is going to be forgiven, released, accepted, understood and received (in other words, if the flight attendant is going to be forgiven for overlooking something that inconvenienced me), God isn't going to administrate it. I have to do it.

What will motivate me to do so, especially if I don't like 1) what happened, 2) how I was accused, 3) the argument that was thrown at me or 4) the inconvenience of injustice I suffered? As I said earlier, I will only give over, forgive or release when I remember how vastly greater than my frustration or pain are the dimensions of God's forgiveness toward me. That's the "key" to the Key, if you will.

Jesus puts this key in our hands through a story designed

to prompt the spirit of God's "release" through us. And we will be called upon to show that spirit toward others in many kinds of situations:

- Toward former friends who hurt our feelings or who failed to keep our trust with a private matter

- Toward an unfaithful spouse who stumbled miserably but who now in genuine repentance and humility has asked to be received again

- Toward Christians whose doctrinal positions disagree with yours and who speak critically or unkindly against you as if you don't love Christ Jesus as they do

- Toward someone who made you look bad when you were in no wise responsible for the failing for which they blamed you

- Toward someone who refused to affirm your innocence

- Toward the irresponsible person who owes you and doesn't pay (It's *not* wrong to expect repayment. It *is* wrong to become embittered when unpaid.)

Take a survey this coming week of each occasion when something nags, bothers or irritates you — when someone or something comes to mind that rankles you or conjures memories of pain, anger or breached relationship. Into each incident breathe the question: "Is the other person's need of my understanding greater than the degree of patience or understanding I needed and need from God?" Obviously, any answer which would claim a private privilege for keeping my hurt or hostile feelings toward another person or group can only demonstrate failure to come to terms with three things:

1. The depth of my own need in the past (and the reality of my continuing need in the present) for the mercy and grace of God's kindness to be shown to me, notwithstanding my sinfulness.

2. The greatness of God's gift of love (His Son), Christ's gift of redemption (His life) and the Spirit's gift of grace (bringing me to Christ).

3. The responsibility you and I have to administrate and maintain a gracious, forgiving, loving and accepting relationship with others. God settled accounts between Himself and me by His action. He holds me responsible to administrate my accounts with others in that light — but it's *my* set of accounts to keep.

These are items to inventory in myself whenever I'm tempted to take on "excess baggage."

The Penalty

We've discussed the ungrateful servant's problem. Now we move on to his penalty.

And his master was angry, and delivered him to the torturers until he should pay all that was due to him (v. 34).

Please notice what is and what isn't said. What *isn't* said is that the man was returned to his former state. Remember that he originally was to lose everything he had, including freedom and family. Now he simply loses the peace of mind which attends debts that are cleared. The "torturers" mentioned here were not a group of legally commissioned sadists whose job was to stretch people on racks until they changed their attitudes. No, they were nagging bill collectors, agents regularly appearing at the door to extract payments.

Let's be clear on this point. Jesus is *not* suggesting, "If you don't forgive as you've been forgiven with the hope of heaven, then the deal is off, and you're going to hell." What He is saying is something which physicians have always suspected and, in this technologically advanced day, have been able to study and verify: People who don't forgive tend to be sick.

This doesn't mean that all sick people are unforgiving. What it does reveal is that multitudes of human afflictions are directly traceable to the long-term impact of bitterness, anger, resentment, hatred or animosity on the human frame. They're all forms of unforgiveness. The fact is that the structure of our human bodies and personalities were not created to bear the burden of unforgiveness. The body, heart, mind, emotions — in part or in whole — will "crack" under the weight of an abiding spirit of un-forgiving-ness. So the text reminds us of the desirability of *not* putting oneself back in the mode of carrying what God has intended to relieve us of.

Think of it! A man once forgiven of all his debt is now making payments again by reason of his smallness of soul! That's the lesson Jesus taught. It isn't a message of renounced salvation but of refused peace. Peace of heart, mind, soul and body can only be enjoyed when God's forgiveness is transmitted *through* us as fully as it has been given *to* us.

If I refuse to be a channel for God's loving spirit of release, the backwash of my bitterness will create a septic tank of foul unforgiveness and a breeding place for Beelzebub's flies. Or if I let the cholesterol-like particles of personal pettiness accumulate in my soul's veins, I may end up spiritually comatose — completely out of touch with the world around me. Like a victim of a spiritual stroke or heart attack, I haven't let my mind be as Christ's or my heart beat as His. I missed *giving* in His order of gracious largeness of heart.

The Pronouncement

The pronouncement from the Savior's lips seals this parable in place. Referring to the lost joy and the continuing, nagging debt which the master allowed to be inflicted upon the unforgiving servant, Jesus says:

> So My heavenly Father also will do to you if each of you, from his heart, does not forgive his brother his trespasses (Matt. 18:35).

It's a resounding restatement of the words which He speaks immediately after having taught His disciples the prayer-paradigm which we refer to as the Lord's Prayer:

> For if you forgive men their trespasses, your heavenly Father will also forgive you. But if you do not forgive men their trespasses, neither will your Father forgive your trespasses (Matt. 6:14-15).

It's a heavenly voice thundering wisdom across the years: Don't forget to forgive! Don't return to joyless living by becoming a forgetful servant. You have been forgiven. Now live forgivingly. Give *up* your claim to being "right." Give *over* your burden of bitterness to God. Give *in* to the Holy Spirit's correction when tempted not to forgive.

Giving — it's the Key to Everything!

- *For*giving keeps the soul and body healthy.
- *For*giving allows reconciled relationships.
- *For*giving maintains gratitude for God's grace.
- *For*giving opens prison doors and releases life.

Let me give you an example.

FOUR

A GUY NAMED JOE

*I realized that my giving
(in his case, forgiving)
may well determine
the degree of release
in the spiritual realm
for others — a release
needed to move
people into alignment
with God's purposes
for them.*

I'VE TOLD about Joe on every continent but Antarctica. I've even written about him in another of my books. But I *must* incorporate the story of a guy named Joe into this book because it speaks of life's possibilities for success or failure — how we process family relationships.

Shortly after Anna and I were married, we went to the Nebraska plains where she had been raised as the near-youngest of nine children. This was my initiating visit with her family, and that's when I met Joe. Most of the family received me warmly, but I picked up a low-grade rejection from Joe, and I understood it.

Joe was away from God.

Though he'd been raised as a Christian, Joe distanced

himself from anyone whom he felt might possibly crowd his chosen lifestyle. Understanding that, I did nothing to make him feel that I was on a crusade for his soul. In fact, I simply chose to treat him as a brother — accepting him, whatever he chose to do. Of course, I would like to have seen him return to a walk with Christ, but I wasn't going to make him feel pushed. So there was no reason for Joe to be less brotherly to me than I was to him, even though I was a relative who, being in training for the ministry, might seem threatening.

Over the first years I worked at winning Joe's friendship, but he wouldn't crack — not even slightly. I thought his coolness would wear away with time, but he always retained that relational distance, notwithstanding the warmest of overtures I made in different, attempting-to-be-brotherly ways.

Then the turning point came. It wasn't good.

It was fifteen years into my acquaintance with Joe when Anna, our kids and I made a trip back to Nebraska to celebrate her folks' fiftieth wedding anniversary. It was a heartwarming time, with friends and family gathered from all points of the compass.

In that setting, I was out in the backyard talking to Joe one day. As we conversed, his cool reserve seemed again, as so often before, to be measuring me as though we had never met.

Sensing that attitude *again* was "the straw that broke it" for me. Something very unobservable outwardly, yet very real within me, snapped. It was my closing a door, my exercising a private, unspoken decision resulting from years of becoming tired and impatient with Joe's attitude — his almost snobbish air of rejection. I'd never felt it from anyone else, so I knew it wasn't paranoia on my part but rather a very real resistance on his part to common decency.

This day I simply decided on the spot, "I'm through trying!" That's all it was; I was just plain tired of trying. And though I didn't physically walk away from him at that moment, in attitude I did. I was through making the effort at friendliness with Joe. I'd tried long and hard enough! "He doesn't care," I thought, "and I don't need to put up with his 'drippy' unresponsiveness anymore!"

Summer and autumn passed that year. And on one overcast Valentine's Day morning back home in California, God stabbed me with a truth and understanding. Looking back, I can see that I was entirely oblivious to my need. Joe was far from my mind, and I felt entirely justified for determining to be as indifferent to our relationship as he was. I hadn't thought about that summertime decision since the moment it occurred, but it was all about to come crashing around my head with dynamic spiritual impact.

As I strolled into the kitchen, my eye was caught by a Valentine card lying on the table. I flipped it open, having read the front page which was a setup for what I expected to be a funny punch line. But the joke turned out to be on me! I don't remember the punch line printed in the card, but I'll never forget the words written at the bottom. They were penned by Joe's daughter, who had sent the card to our daughter Becki. The two teenage girls had struck up a nice friendship, even though their growing up together was half a continent apart.

The words read: "Dear Becki, I just wanted to add a note to thank you for mentioning in your last letter that you are regularly praying for my dad to come back to Jesus."

That's when the "stabbing" occurred.

The Holy Spirit jabbed me awake to two things. The first was the unworthiness of my counter-rejection of attitude toward Joe. God used my daughter to jar me to an awareness that two teenagers were exchanging mutual concern and sharing prayer for a man I had the unholy, blinded audacity to "give up on." Worse, I awakened to a second humbling fact.

Don't ask me to try to explain why because I did care about Joe's soul, and I *was* pursuing faithful ministry during all the intervening years. But the truth is that in the fifteen years I had known him, to my sudden awareness, I could not remember even once having prayed specifically for Joe!

Go ahead and ask me: "Why, Jack! What? Never prayed for him? Didn't you care about him — at least, until that summer decision?"

And the only answer I can give is yes, I cared. But apparently something about my attitude regarding his rejecting ways toward me had blocked me from recognizing my own neglect. But now, this Valentine morning, the Spirit of God was birthing a repentance and a love in my heart.

I literally fell to my knees there, alone in the kitchen, and I wept. I repented for my blindness, for my hardheartedness, for my impatience and for my "signing off" on Joe. I asked God's forgiveness for the prayerlessness my attitude had begotten in me. And I prayed for Joe. I prayed with an entirely new sense of love for the man, for his soul, for "Joe, no matter how he is — I care, Lord!" And I really did.

Time went by. My heart had mellowed, and love for Joe — without any return from him — was real. Then came the day.

It was the next August, following the Valentine's Day "massacre" of the spirit of my unforgivingness. That Sunday night Anna and I had come home from church. The kids had gone to their rooms to prepare for bed, Anna to the kitchen for a snack and I to the bedroom to change into something more relaxing. The phone rang.

It was Joe. "Hi, guys!" he greeted us brightly as Anna and I both picked up extensions simultaneously. He didn't take long to get to the point.

"Jack, Anna, I just wanted to call you both tonight because I felt you would want to be among the first to know. I came back to the Lord today!" He was jubilant. He was free.

And I was weeping, laughing and praising God at the same time!

We visited for several minutes and then concluded the call. It was a holy reunion around the throne of God. But when the call was over, I lay back on the pillow in our bedroom, praying thoughtfully, "Lord, could it be that my unrecognized attitude of judging Joe because he was rejecting me had somehow 'bound' him away from a spiritual breakthrough until I became forgiving and lovingly prayerful?"

I didn't receive an answer. But I later discovered in the parable of the unforgiving servant how the story ends with the servant left in the debtors' prison.

Now please know that I realize that each person is responsible for his or her own relationship to God. And also know that it's not my desire to impose guilt on you, as though the goal of this insight is to hold either you or me responsible for every person who doesn't make his or her own responsible choice for Christ. But there is something of substance here regarding our ability to "bind" or "loose" one another as human beings.

We accept this fact already in some respects. For example, we do accept responsibility for whether some people enter God's kingdom. Sure we do! How many times have we given to an evangelistic or missionary ministry "so that souls may be reached and saved." We accept the terms of that appeal: Only as we give will souls be released. And in that light, honesty requires our acknowledgment: It may *also* be that my *for*giving is equally as important as my *giving*.

Suddenly I was seeing the awesome reality within this truth, and Joe's return to the good Shepherd's fold had opened my eyes. I can't prove it, but the evidence is there to examine as a very valid possibility: Joe didn't return until I learned to forgive. It's parallel to the "missions" proposition above: Many people can't be *reborn* until you and I *give*.

Of course, I'd rather avoid the implication of this possible truth, which holds me liable for lost people if I'm unforgiving toward them. It's so much easier to give money than to forgive people. But the whole concept of the sameness of giving — whether the mercy of forgiveness or the resource of money — began to dawn on my understanding. Giving as the Key to Everything became just a little clearer to my perspective. I was seeing more clearly the matter of responsibility in my stewardship of what I've received:

- I've received God's love: I owe it to others.

  Therefore, since I've received it gladly, I am to transmit it gladly.

- I've received the gift of life-breath: I owe its use to God.

  Therefore, since my life-breath is a gift, I'm to use it to praise God and never to speak negatively of His creatures.

- I've received strength to work and the blessing of income. Both are gifts to me.

  Therefore, having received of God's hand, I'll handle my money in obedience to Him and in the interest of His kingdom.

The experience of seeing what happened to Joe when I began to exercise proper stewardship over my heart's attitude was too close to a reality I'd never seen. I realized that my giving (in his case, *forgiving*) may well determine the degree of release in the spiritual realm for others — a release needed to move people into alignment with God's purposes for them.

While I shuddered to think of the implications of that

possibility, I couldn't escape it. Theologize, rationalize, debate or argue — the bottom line was still the same: My giving in any part of my life integrates with the other parts. I knew there was no way that passivity could be allowed. While I like far better the idea that "God will take over and cover whatever I don't do — after all, that's what grace is all about," I doubted it was true. That's because grace isn't about God's compensatory covering for neglect or indifference; it's only about ignorance and inability. Yes, He does cover what we don't see, understand or do. But He isn't one to issue licenses for what I *won't* do.

Progressively, the redeemed-forgiven child of God needs to grow to accept this fact — and respond to it. There is no division between these two expressions of life's flow — mercy and money, forgiveness and finance. It is one of the most falacious and destructive dichotomies formed by human reasonings. Moving the material realm apart from the spiritual, we too easily attempt to frame neat compartments which will remove our responsibility for linking them in our living. But the Word of God calls us to a literal accounting — and remember, *accounting* is a financial/bookkeeping term. You and I are accountable for both

- how we steward the forgiveness we've received and

- how we manage the money which comes into our hands.

We're not allowed to clutch money or forgiveness to ourselves, as though their benefits were simply for our enjoyment without transmittal to others. To sum it up:

1. I started to learn about giving on a flight to Portland.

2. That lesson helped me understand more about it from the lips of Jesus through a kingdom parable.

3. Discovering my apparently restrictive behavior regarding Joe moved me further along the line of learning how giving is the Key to Everything.

Now let's look at instances of this being put into practice.

FIVE

Two for
the Money

*In God's financial
order, giving is not
just an end in itself...
Everything is affected by
the spirit of giving.*

THE YEAR Anna and I entered ministry, we began the task of planting a new church in Indiana. The little building we started in (it measured only thirty-six by twenty-four feet!) had originally been a school built just outside the city limits. But with the passage of time, the city had grown up around it, and, unimpressive as it appeared, this was the building to which a young, just-out-of-Bible-college couple was commissioned to establish a new congregation.

It was slow — very slow. But after a while, a few people began to attend, and gradually some came to Christ. However, being completely new in the Lord and lacking a church background, they all had to be taught the Bible's basic foundational truths of practical living in the Lord's way.

One day we were talking with Earl and Dorothy, a couple who was really beginning to mature, hungry to grow up in Christ. They had known the Lord for only a short time, but they were excited and eager, pursuing the new life they had found and ready to follow with all their hearts.

That evening, Anna and I had stopped by Earl and Dorothy's house to visit. After we had sat down in the living room, Earl reached over to hand me an orange card. Even as he was doing so, you could see a sparkle of real joy in his eyes.

"I just wanted you to see this," he said, smiling.

I immediately recognized the card because everyone in town received one every month. It was the bill from the water and power department. I took the card and looked at the balance due as Earl continued to talk.

"As you know, Dorothy and I have begun to seek to walk with a real commitment to the Lord in all the areas of our lives," he said. "One of the things we know we need to do is to begin giving God's way. Since you've taught us the biblical patterns and practices of giving, we believe we're to obey — to step out by faith and start — *now*."

He explained further: "We've never built a plan of giving into our budget, and we know that if we *wait* to get started, it will probably never happen. So we decided to *commit* — just to take the step and trust God to keep His Word."

I was touched by the happiness he was manifesting as he spoke. It was such a tender evidence of true, childlike faith, unspoiled by religious legalism.

"That's great, Earl," I said, "but what is it you two want Anna and me to pray about?"

"Well," he replied, "we want to start by at least giving a tithe. We don't have enough in this week's budget to do that, but we are going to anyway. Now this is the bill we're not able to pay. As I said, we've decided to start giving — *now*."

He smiled again, but he didn't seem to be nervous, uneasy or trying to act spiritual. In fact, to the contrary, they both seemed to be filled with the joy of obedience and clearly at ease in that rest which only comes from a genuine trust in God that is born of faith in His Word.

However, *my* response was another matter!

The words he had just spoken were echoing in my ears: "You have taught us we should do this."

Suddenly I felt frighteningly responsible! What if God didn't meet this need in time? What if their lights were turned off because of something I'd taught? What if Earl and Dorothy's faith-growth was stunted as a result of *me?*

I had this sudden, churning fear that inconvenience or injury might happen to someone because of what I had taught. I also (foolishly, of course) felt that my reputation (and maybe even *God's!*) was at stake. Immediately I began to pray silently in quiet desperation: "O Lord! If ever You answered a prayer, answer this one here!"

This sudden burst of fear didn't last long, however, because with almost equal immediacy I regained my emotional and spiritual equilibrium. Since I had been taught from childhood to give faithfully, I knew from the earliest years of my life how God provides for those who give in obedient faith. So I set aside my fearful concerns, and we prayed.

"Father, thank You! Thank You for Earl and Dorothy's trust in Your promise. We look to You to fulfill the need they've expressed by reason of the budgeted monies displaced by their taking this faith-step in giving as Your Word teaches us. We place the need in Your hands, just as surely as their gift has been put in Your hands. Thank You for taking care of this. In Jesus' name, amen."

I felt free to pray with confidence, not only because of my own history of seeing God provide, but because they had such a peace.

I had not constrained them to do this. I had made no legal demands. I had not made promises of sudden wealth. I had only taught God's Word.

And they believed it!

I'll bet you know what happened, too.

About two weeks later, Dorothy caught us in passing to tell how some unexpected monies had come to them — "coincidentally" being exactly what they needed! Of course, it was a tremendously thrilling, faith-building event for the two new converts, but it was for me, too. It was a holy reminder not only of God's commitment to support His Word, but of His timeliness in confirming it as well.

Turned on to Giving

Let me add a second story to Earl and Dorothy's.

It was quite a few years later, and Anna and I were pastoring The Church On The Way, as we still are. In the short number of years we had been here, a real visitation of God's divine grace had come. Suddenly the little church had grown from about 18 members to 100, and then from 100 to 750. Because so many of these were young in Christ as Earl and Dorothy had been, I knew I needed to teach them about giving also. Yet I felt hesitant because many of those who had come to Christ were young people who had come out of countercultural backgrounds laden with anti-authoritarian attitudes.

It was the early 1970s, and in North America we were still working through the "hippie era." A few of these newly saved people had grown up in churches but had become reactionary to features of church traditions that their parents had embraced — traditions in which there had been observances without vitality, religious habits without real holiness.

There were also others in the congregation who had real financial tangles in their lives due to their checkered pasts. They didn't seem ready to realize that the way to get financially untangled was to line up with God's financial order — to learn financial giving on His terms.

These new Christians were willing to give, at least to a degree, but it still was clearly on their terms. And they obviously preferred that no one was too direct in talking about money in church. To teach boldly on giving would have appeared to them as being legalistic or as "too churchy" and not "gently Christian." To their idealized views, straight talk about money — even by God — could somehow de-sanctify the beauty of giving from the heart or interrupt the simple joy of liberated living, which for some of these dear young believers was still subject to their definition of *free*.

I knew, of course, that I wasn't going to communicate legalistically or lovelessly, but still I didn't want to be misunderstood as reverting to any appearance of dead, traditional ways which had "turned off" a generation of youth. Thus, I found myself in a quandary as to how I could balance these two things: 1) my *responsibility* as a teacher of the Word with 2) the appropriate *sensitivity* which I felt was necessary given the history and mood among many of my growing congregation.

I decided to do what I have done all of my life: *teach God's Word*. But I asked the Lord for a special favor.

As I began preparing the message series on giving, I prayed, "Lord, as I teach this series on giving, I ask that You would not only cause understanding to come to those who hear, but please do another thing. Because I believe Your whole Word throbs with saving life, let that life — even in the subject of giving — breathe understanding into the hearts of people who need You. Lord, I pray, cause people to be saved *even as I teach on tithing!* Though salvation and forgiveness aren't the main thrust of my first sermon in the series, I ask you to confirm Your Word of truth with souls coming to salvation. Amen."

God Responds

It was astounding! As I taught that first Sunday, the Lord blessed the Word. That morning *more than thirty people received Christ!* It had happened again: God's pleasure and readiness to confirm His Word in every way were manifest, even when the truths of financial obedience to God were taught!

Needless to say, I was tremendously comforted, being reminded once again that in God's financial order, giving is not just an end in itself. That instance was another early demonstration, teaching me clearly how much *everything* is affected by the spirit of giving.

These stories combine to show how in teaching us to *give*, God can bring us all

- *to new levels of understanding and obedience,* as He did with Earl and Dorothy;

- *to new points of faith and assurance,* as He did with my young congregation; and

- *to new moments of life and joy,* as He did with those who received Jesus Christ as I committed to teach about giving even when it seemed difficult.

There is one basic key to this kind of living.
Here it is.

SIX

THE
MASTER'S
KEY

*Our human capacity
to receive is functional
in direct proportion to
our capacity to give;
but our capacity to
receive is dysfunctional
in direct proportion to
our desperate need to get.*

I T WAS one of the most exciting "possibility moments" in
my young life — and I choked. That is, my emotions
were so excited they jammed and virtually immobilized
my powers of thought.

It was Thanksgiving Day. And along with other guests and
family, my Aunt Margaret had arrived. She was a woman of a
rather queenly disposition: gracious and loving, but borne
along on something of an air of royalty — dignified and
noble. Her husband, who had died some years before, had
been the mayor of the small Midwestern city where she had
lived for years, and something of being "first lady" never
quite left her. She was wonderful.

And this Thanksgiving, "wonderful" was about to reach

new proportions because Aunt Margaret had just grouped the three of us kids in a corner of the living room — my brother, sister and me — and made an offer.

"Children," she began grandiosely, "it's Thanksgiving, and I want you to tell me everything you can — as long a list as you wish — everything for which you feel thankful today. And for every single thing you are able to think of, I'm going to give you fifty cents!"

Before you read further, I want to ask you to pause with me and evaluate this moment.

Not only is fifty cents still a significant amount of money for a schoolchild, but in terms of the relative value of U. S. currency when this offer was made, this was *real* money. Aunt Margaret was a fairly well-to-do woman, and she wasn't offering peanuts. In the values of the 1940s, we would be looking at something a little closer to five bucks a crack! I'm talkin' big money!

There I stood on the brink of eternal wealth. My economic senses set my emotional juices pumping at a rate sufficient to skyrocket my mind to hyperspace proportions — Fort Knox being in immediate view.

And I froze.

Absolutely couldn't think.

I fumbled, I sputtered and I struggled with such gargantuan possibilities and managed to come up with "Mama," "Daddy," "our house" and "our family." It's a sad commentary on anyone's imagination regardless of age. Today I can think of mega-millions of things. How about *Aunt Margaret* — for starters — and then, her *fingers*, her *toes* (that's twenty times fifty cents right there) and so on into infinity!

I ended up getting a measly two bucks! It's an unforgettable day of missed opportunity.

Whenever I think of *abundance* as a possibility, that episode from my early life comes to mind. There's something very telling about that story, for it reaches to the core of a basic blockage which is potential in us all. Let me cast it in something of a Murphy's law:

> Our human capacity to receive is functional in direct proportion to our capacity to *give*; but our capacity to receive is dysfunctional in direct proportion to our desperate need to *get*.
>
> *Hayford's Law of the Aunt-Margaret*
> *Thanksgiving-Day Crash and Burn*

To be brief: I couldn't *give* thanks because my young mind was so preoccupied with *getting*. The possibility of getting a half-dollar a head for my "thankfuls" crippled my "thank-thinker." And as simple as the story may be, at its root is a fundamental problem soaked deep into our human nature. It's the problem Jesus was seeking to solve permanently in our spirits and dissolve in terms of bondage, when He declared what I call the Master's Key:

> Give, and it will be given to you: good measure, pressed down, shaken together, and running over will be put into your bosom (Luke 6:38a).

In these words, Jesus — the Master — has given us a summary of God's total-life plan of release. It transcends money matters, though it includes them, and to capture its spirit is to lay hold of the Master's Key. It is to enter the realm of learning to give in the spirit of God's heart for giving, rather than merely learning lip service to the letter of God's laws. Genuine understanding makes the difference.

Growing in knowing God's heart will cultivate *true* giving in the spirit of God's release. This will move us beyond humanly formulated, regimented programs, however biblically conceived.

Joyous, praise-filled giving (born of prayer and the Spirit instead of promotion and the systems) brings great giving alive and propels its possibilities of release forward. Growing, knowing, seeing and giving in beat with the heart of Jesus will steer past dead tradition on one hand and past charges of "health-wealth gospelism" on the other. Why? Because giving becomes rooted in the *spirit* of Jesus' own words. Look at the text you read earlier, and let's scrutinize each phrase.

Give, and it will be given to you.

First, let's unapologetically accept one thing: though this verse may relate to monetary giving (and has been proven as an economic principle), it should *not* be confined to money matters in our understanding. As we've seen, the whole concept of giving is as wide as all of life. So, as we study the Master's Key, let us keep the *dual dimensions* of its message in perspective: It bears on *living* as well as *giving*.

Next, note these words:

Put into your bosom.

This can probably be made clearer to our understanding by employing such phrases as "shall be *heaped* into your robe" or "*piled* into your lap." The picture is of a person seated and of an abundance poured in such a way it would end up spilling all over him!

The words *into your bosom* literally refer to the upper part of the torso, relating to the design of people's garments in Jesus' time. Men generally secured their robe-like clothing with a belt around the waist in a way that made a giant pocket formed by the fold in the upper part of the garment. Jesus is saying, "When your *hand* gives from the *heart*, you'll experience a robe-full of returned blessing."

Without a doubt He means real material resource is involved — literal, physical things. But the image contains more. There's no way to escape the intended picture the old word *bosom* brings to mind. It seems Jesus means us also to know that a *heart-full* of blessing will be forthcoming to the giver — flooding his heart spiritually and flowing forth his reward materially. Jesus is noting how giving enlarges the heart and makes room for more to be poured into it.

The book of Ruth provides us with an illustration of this idea. In the story, Boaz, who is a marvelous Old Testament picture of our Lord Jesus Christ, has revealed his love for Ruth, an equally beautiful picture of the church, that is, of you and me. As they are about to become engaged, Boaz expresses his commitment to Ruth by asking her to spread out her shawl (see Ruth 3:15-18). Into its folds he pours out six ephahs of grain — a total of about seventy pounds of barley!

It's always struck me as rather amusing that the man stacked seventy pounds of *anything* on his bride-to-be! But beyond the homeliness of the act, see how this "little token" of his love for her was a real evidence of the abundance of love he wanted to pour out on her (not to mention that it shows that Ruth was a pretty sturdy girl!).

Now catch the picture. Can you see our Lord Jesus saying the same thing to us, His bride? "I don't want you to go through life empty-handed. I want you to know My abounding provision for *all* matters of your life."

In short, Jesus Christ is saying, "I will fill the biggest pocket you've got! I'll fill it with love and all you need to live as well."

That's His promise!

He wants to give us as much as we can hold, not for accumulation of selfish or personal gain, but for supplying our lives, for providing for our families and for filling our ministries with love and power. God's giving plan is never short-sighted and not to be short-circuited. Jesus' next words make that very clear.

For with the same measure that you use, it will be measured back to you (Luke 6:38b).

Without fear or apology we need to describe this exactly for what it says: This is the *reciprocal law of giving*. That is, when you give something, something will come back to you. And the inverse is equally true: If you don't give, you lose, for there will be no return.

Of course, Jesus isn't trying to bribe us to give. He isn't saying, "You'll get a little prize in the box if you buy My cereal." Instead, He wants us to understand that life does not work without our welcoming the spirit of giving. He's saying, "Learn to give greatly because great living ensues upon great giving." This principle applies to every area of life.

- People don't have friends because they don't offer friendship.

- People can't establish pure relationships because they don't apply God's pure terms to the conduct of the relationships they're pursuing.

- People don't *feel* forgiven because they won't *give* forgiveness.

- People don't find contentment because they won't accept God's providence.

The principle of reciprocity — of an expected return for giving — is *God's* idea for expanding life's dimensions through giving. Giving money, giving kindness, giving time, giving up, giving in, giving "givingly"!

It's not surprising that critics say, "The only reason people such as you talk and urge 'giving' is because of what you think you'll get back." But don't be stalled or distracted by these petty critics. When God opens the door of a promise, some cynic will be ready to slam it closed. Sooner or later, no matter how beautiful a truth God gives, you'll hear someone express it in a way that confuses and cheapens the beauty of its simplicity. But these things notwithstanding, let us not back away from this life-principle of reciprocal giving. Jesus is the One who has declared it, and you and I can welcome its promise and expect its reward as we joyfully give in faith's spirit of love!

Notice, too, there's a matching principle tied to the law of reciprocity. It's the *law of self-administrated return*: "With the measure you measure, it shall be measured to you."

It's uncanny.

Whether we like it or not, Jesus says that *we* are the ones who will determine if God's abundance will flow toward us. We are the ones who will choose whether or not we:

- "open the door" (and receive His loving promise) or

- "turn on the faucet" (and release an inward flow of grace and gifts that allow our outward flow of service or giving).

In other words, *ours* is to open the way for *His* overflow to be released. The Master's Key to living and giving is placed in our hands. He pointedly declares that our knowledgeable and discerning response in giving is essential to allow the bounty of God's blessing into all the situations in our lives.

These truths are *so* promising, but they are also *so* exacting.

The reciprocal promise and the self-administrated limits — these principals are so enormous in potential and so demanding in discipline that we could be tempted to avoid them. Or to deny their simple, direct reality. Or to pooh-pooh their promises. Or to flee the responsibility they call us to. They converge to form so mighty a key that we need to be reminded again: Our giving has nothing to do with our salvation or ultimate relationship with God. These lessons on giving present nothing of a "works" program because our *learning* to give has nothing to do with our *earning* God's pleasure.

But giving does have to do with seeking to learn God's ways! And while we don't have to *earn* His pleasure in order to be saved, we do need to *learn* His ways in order to grow in abundant living.

Those "abundant ways" are the "teeth" in the Key to Everything. Let me explain what I mean.

SEVEN

BROADENING THE BLESSING

*How I give
inevitably impacts
how I live — and
how I view and
relate to people.*

YOU'VE HAD it happen to you.

You go to have a key made. You pay the clerk, head for home and put the newly ground key into the lock. Nothing.

You pull it out — check to see if it's the right one. Try again. And no amount of pushing, pulling, sliding, "try-to" turning or twisting does a thing.

Something was missed. It was one of those tiny "teeth" — the notches in the key which permit or prohibit the key to turn the lock mechanism. If only one "tooth" is missing, you're locked out.

There's a message here somewhere! And it's crucial to not finding myself "locked out" of a part of my life because I didn't allow God's Spirit to grind out any part of me that would block His blessing. The Master's Key, as we've studied it, carries "giving" all the way to the most practical issues of life. In doing so, Jesus spells out the issues that "put the teeth into" the Key to Everything. What's He up to here?

The Master's Motive

First, Jesus Christ's mightiest work in any of us is the salvation of our souls. That priority is never in question. But as we begin to probe the dimensions of the new life He's birthed in us, it soon becomes clear that He's very desirous of doing more than saving us.

God not only wants to save our souls, He wants to help us make life *work*. He has come to enable us to *"reign in life"* (Rom. 5:17). That's what He means when He says that He has come that we might have life "more abundantly" (John 10:10). He's seeking to direct us into a life that functions effectively in everything, at every time and in every place. That's why the Master focuses us on His Key to Everything with these words which call us to *relay* everything we've *received*:

Freely you have received, freely give (Matt. 10:8).

His objective is "release" — to release our *living* to its maximum potential by calling forth our *giving* to its fullest possibilities.

In His summary Key (Luke 6:38), Jesus so thoroughly integrates giving with life that He makes this an inescapable fact: Only as we learn to *give* are we learning to *live*.

Now in the adjacent verse (Luke 6:37), more specific requirements are put into the "giving" process. He has made giving far more than a money matter — it's a *life issue*, and in four brief phrases He calls for a broad-based application of the spirit of giving. It's His way of teaching us that a set of issues (circumstances/attitudes/moods) must be dealt with in order to broaden the base of the blessing potential in giving. In listing these expectations — and indeed, they are *demands* for us to use the Key to Everything — He puts the "teeth" into the Key.

- Judge not, and you shall not be judged.

- Condemn not, and you shall not be condemned.

- Forgive, and you will be forgiven.

- Give, and it will be given to you (Luke 6:37-38a).

Look closely. Don't miss anything on the list.

A missing tooth in a key — or in a smile — can be an embarrassing thing!

The matters Jesus has mentioned here — all pivotal attitudes which affect daily words and actions — are linked to the text which enunciates His Master Key. Luke 6:38, which we've examined already, is too often applied only to finances. But these four "teeth" put the bite on us: *Judge not. Condemn not. Forgive. Give.* They demand a practical, daily application of giving in more ways than we customarily perceive as essential to the spirit of giving.

These four statements touch the core of everything that has to do with life — our relationships and our resources. The challenge Jesus issues requires us to let Him stretch and grow us. That's not easy because our natural human tendency is to shrink and stagnate, not stretch and grow. Just as a garment can shrink to a fraction of its size by going through the washer's wetness and the dryer's heat, our souls can shrink in the turbulent waters of life's sea and the heat of life's pressures.

How easily we succumb to judging, condemning and to unforgiveness. But by letting the truth of God's Word and the presence of Jesus work in us to *stretch* the fabric of our souls, a largeness of life will open. First it will open up *in* us, then its bounty can open out *through* us.

So many things change when we grow in the true spirit of giving, that is, in the "spirit of God's release." The bitterness of criticism, the pettiness of judgmentalism, the quickness to condemn and the slowness to forgive — *all* will be crowded out by our committing to giving place to a holy largess of loving and giving.

Then, look at how Jesus ties the graces of our growth in character to our habits and attitudes about our finances.

Giving That Doesn't Give In

It was another one of those days when Jesus was confronted by the religious crowd. Here He's arguing with the Pharisees, showing them that even a person's faithfulness in giving is no substitute for their growth and purity of character.

> Woe to you, scribes and Pharisees, hypocrites! For you pay tithe of mint and anise and cummin, and have neglected the weightier matters of the law: justice and mercy and faith. These you ought to have done, without leaving the others undone (Matt. 23:23).

Catch the irony here! It's evident when we list this set of facts: The scribes and the Pharisees

1. exploited their wives,

2. were completely indifferent to their marriage vows,

3. were looking for ways to legally divorce one wife and marry another,

4. disdained the dearest of human relationships and

5. were always interested in verifying their own righteousness, *but...*

they always paid their tithes!

Weird, isn't it? Tithing to the penny, yet puny in their souls. What's the message? It is this: that there is a kind of "giving" that hasn't really learned to "give in" to God.

The pointed truth in this scene is that God views any giving which is only a legalistic performance as useless — unacceptable. Financial giving must be matched with a commitment to God's love, life and values, or the *life* in giving withers. When the joy and love in giving are absent, its power evaporates.

For example, how many people do you suppose have assumed that if they give — even tithe — they have exempted themselves from other points of growth in God's grace? They tithe at church, but hate at home. It's like saying to God, "I gave at the office;" therefore, they conclude that *living* in a giving spirit is "unnecessary" at home or the office or wherever.

And somehow, such formalism as this "I-already-gave" excuse can subtly remove people's availability to allowing God to purify further, to refine or deepen their practicing His love and ways. Or it can even block their availability for expanded giving financially! Look how that seems to have happened to these Pharisees.

It's interesting to note that while Jesus commended the *tithes* of the Pharisees, He made no mention of their *offerings*. Is there an insight here? Are we looking at people who religiously adhered to the "duty" of tithing, but only obeyed this as a legal obligation? And were offerings — revelatory of expanding love and generosity — not even practiced?

I think that's what happened.

The Lord Jesus is doing two things here: confronting small-souled attitudes and challenging large-hearted gratitude. He's saying, "Learn to 'let go' in *all* your life!"

Jesus' purpose in these four "teeth" commands — don't judge, don't condemn, do forgive and do give — is to move us beyond Pharisee-like smallness. The same smallness of heart that manifests in judgmentalism, condemnation and unforgiveness can also cause us to live in stinginess or in the fear of giving. So it is that our Lord sets the issue of giving in perspective, showing that it touches the core of all life's relationships. How I *give* inevitably impacts how I *live* — and how I view and relate to people.

A "Mobile Beer Bust"

Recently, in the middle of the night, I woke up to the sound of many car doors slamming and other cars cruising back and forth, up and down, our street. I got up, went to the front window and peeked out to discover that about a dozen cars had pulled up in front of my house and our neighbors' houses. People were getting out and wandering around — talking to each other loudly and laughing drunkenly. All this activity was clearly unrelated to anybody in the neighborhood — it wasn't a local party.

I observed the proceedings for a few minutes to see what was going on, and before many minutes had gone by I figured it out. A "mobile beer bust" was going on — right in front of my house — in fact, some of it right on my lawn! I felt it was too risky to go out there and say anything; frankly, I would have been afraid to. So I just returned to bed and went back to sleep since the group didn't seem violent and there wasn't anything to be done.

When I got up in the morning and looked out of the window, I saw pretty much what I expected: Trash was everywhere, and beer cans were all over our yard and our neighbors'. It was a mess — and one obviously needing to be cleaned up. So I got a huge garbage bag, went out and started picking up junk.

As I stooped over to pick up the first pieces of trash, I was complaining under my breath, "This is disgusting! The irresponsibility..." (mumble, mumble) "irritating..." (murmur, murmur) "crazy..." I felt anger. But almost instantly the Holy Spirit whispered a different set of words into my ear — *very* unlike the ones on *my* mind:

> Love your enemies, do good to those who hate you,
> bless those who curse you, and pray for those who
> spitefully use you (Luke 6:27-28).

Have you ever wished God would let you have a good "grump" before He corrected your anger? Believe me, this "interruption" by the Spirit's voice sure wasn't prompted by any great nobility on my part.

I was just plain mad.

But at this prompting, I cooled off — fast! And giving the Holy Spirit His place as He was dealing with me, I began to change my mind-set. I started to pray even while I was walking around cleaning up our yard as well as the yards adjacent to ours. It took me about ten to fifteen minutes to pick up all the garbage, but as I prayed during that time, a profound thing happened inside me.

I found my heart moved for the people who did this; who in blind pursuit of meaning, followed foolishness and ended with pointlessness. The thought struck me, "How many people are there *every night* who have hoped to find some fulfillment in a 'big time' and end with admitting, deep in their secret soul, 'There's nothing in this'?"

I was sure some of the very people who had spent part of their night partying on my lawn would feel that exact emotion after waking on this day. And that further moved me to pray for the deluded as well as the disappointed; to pray for those who thought, "Hey, man, this is really living!" I prayed for the Holy Spirit to open eyes, to give revelations that would expose the emptiness of their *real* situations.

I inject this reminscence of my own encounter with my all-too-human readiness to "grump" — to judge, condemn and be angry — in order to relate it to Jesus' point. In short, when Jesus teaches us to give, at the same time He is saying that you and I are to judge not and condemn not. We are to forgive the guy who trashes our lawn; to keep a place in our hearts for anyone who in any other way inconveniences, derides or attacks what you and I live for. Can you see why Jesus makes *giving* such an issue? It's so pivotal for us all, and it becomes the crowning call of this series of commands.

"Give!"

Why is it last on the list?

Because in another sense, it's first.

"Give" is unique among this set of imperatives because it's the only one of the four commands in this text that can be measured.

We can't measure condemnation or even criticism because so much of it is going on inside: it may be verbal, but it's not visible.

And we can't measure forgiveness because there's no visible way to determine how much of it we have or have not shown.

But we *can* measure giving.

You and I both can find out if we're growing in that grace. We *can* measure what's happening in that part of our lives. We can calculate whether we've *tithed* or what amount we've *offered* or how much time we've *served* others. And with this call to give, Jesus calls us to get down to the tangible, the touchable, the real — the inescapably practical. My giving — its literal growth due to a loving spirit — will measurably reflect what's *really* happening in the less measurable, less visible parts of my soul. Chances are, if I'm slow to *give*, I'm also slow to *forgive* — and very likely far too quick to judge, condemn or criticize.

"Give!" That is Jesus' conclusive summons.

As we've said, this doesn't determine whether we go to heaven or not. Grace and glory can't be *bought*. But they are to be *caught!*

They are to *flavor our behavior*, and the truth of the "teeth" in the Master's Key takes Luke 6:37-38 far beyond any shallow notions of "giving to get."

There *is* a promised reward for the giving person, but rather than showing us the way to "getting ours," Christ clearly wants to maximize the release He can work *through* us — in all of our living.

My acceptance or rejection of God's giving program will, in the last analysis, reflect in what kind of a *forgiver*, *non*-condemner or *non*-judger you or I become. Those "teeth" are important if the Key to Everything is going to work — to unlock the future of God's purposes in our lives. A change in our posture toward *people*, as surely as a change in our posture toward our *possessions*, is the goal Jesus has in mind. The result will be a "turnkey" kind of life.

A New Place to Live

"It'll be a turnkey job," the contractor said. What did he mean? He meant that if I'd pay the price, he'd do the work. And he meant that when the job was done, he'd simply hand me the key to a new house — a new place to live.

That's what God's call to giving is all about. It's His offer to us of a new place to live — a new level in life. But there's no avoiding the price: "Give!" That last word in His series of commands which we've called "teeth" is really the cutting edge which completes the pattern revealing the divine design — the Master's Key to Everything.

Measure with me the weight, and sense with me the sharpness in this cutting-edge command: "Give!"

First, please notice the Greek imperative in this text —

87

"*Didote!*" The mode of the verb makes clear that we are not only called to *do*, but to steadfastly, continuously *keep on doing*. Next, having registered His mandate, Jesus follows this command with something so grandly characteristic of God's ways. With the splendor of His holy grace, our Lord beautifully adds promise to precept: Having said, "Give," He adds, "and it will be given to you." He's loving us forward on a pathway of obedience, saying that if we continue on this path in His ways, a blessed promise will be fulfilled.

These words in our text are a watershed point for some supposed purists. I've always been amazed at the number of people who still object to the promise which follows, even though they say they believe the Word of God. They don't like it if you or I accept and teach that Jesus wants to pour out abundance on us by giving back when we give.

They will suggest that we are somehow twisting truth, using this promise as a ploy to get people to give. To enunciate God's loving promise is viewed as though we were pandering to some order of carnal greed in human nature.

But it is *Jesus* who said, "And it will be given!" And He didn't stoop to the level of a shady wheeler-dealer. Jesus isn't beckoning from a dark alley, whispering, "Tell ya' what I'm gonna do. If you'll give in that offering, see, I'm gonna treat ya' good. Now, you *give*, and then I'll give back — *even more!* How does that grab ya'? Whatta deal, hey?"

Maybe I've exaggerated slightly the opposing cynic's voice, but not much. It's sadly amazing that this kind of thinking survives, but listen: This text's promise is not the device of a devious deity — it's His *divine design*.

To teach it isn't to *pander* to flesh, but to *confront* it.

Jesus is showing us something of the way the universe is constructed.

    1. There is a law of reciprocity: "Give, and it will be given to you."

2. Beside it, there is the law of self-determination: "With the same measure that you use, it will be measured back to you."

These two laws converge to bring divine power and promise into immediate contact with human choice and responsibility. Jesus is revealing "all power" available for "all possibilities" — His power and our partnership. He's waiting.

Think of it! God promises that when we open the faucet of possibility through our own giving, a heavenly reservoir is waiting to flow toward us with a whole lot more than you or I could ever contain. But *we* decide how open the faucet will be, and thereby we determine how much of His divine flow will move in our direction.

God doesn't say *He'll* love us more if we open wider, but that *we'll* love more. We become greater people, transformed by the terms of His giving promise, by our allowing Him to flow through us. This greatness is not measured by the *sum*, but by the *spirit*, of our giving. This enlargement breaks us loose from any shrinkage of our souls into a broadness and bigness of Christ's love and life.

That's how Jesus shows giving as the Key to determining a whole lot more than money matters. He shows how it will affect whether we judge, whether we criticize — or whether or not I surrender to anger because garbage is all over my lawn.

This "Give!" is to change us, to grow us *up* past theorizing. In addressing so fundamental an issue as money, God makes it all intensely practical. He helps us recognize more clearly how thoroughly *spiritual* the issues are which come from financial giving and how very practical are the blockages to life's release when the giving spirit is absent.

Money relates to every part of our lives. How we handle it will be a direct reflection of our deepest attitudes, and how we relate to it will determine the quality of our dearest relationships.

Money Translates to "Life"

Money is not life. We all know better than that. And neither is money what life is all about. But there is a proximity of relationship that is so close we dare not miss it. Think about this.

Every time you and I deal with money, we are handling "life." Each dollar we have, each piece of currency that passes through our hands, is in some way directly related to a given amount of someone's life. Why? Because in the present order of things, money is what is given in exchange for a person's time.

It's basic. You, I — everyone — works a certain number of hours at a job. In exchange, a commensurate amount of money is paid at an agreed rate. Life and money are completely integrated. We can take an amount of money paid for an amount of time and literally mean it when we say, "This is *life* in its most practical form."

Again, this isn't to cheapen life's meaning or to say that money is the sum value of life. But we cannot divorce the relationship of money from life. And we can't separate the spiritual significance from either one.

Therefore, when we deal with the issue of giving, we face whether or not we have submitted the *issues* of life to the *Lord* of life. There is hardly a more primary or foundational issue in our lives than money.

It isn't extraneous or unspiritual.

It isn't ethereal or mystical.

But money is very *real*, very *tangible*, very *measurable*, and Jesus makes it *very related* to all life's details.

Money is an inescapable issue, in front of us all the time. And in the face of this most tangible aspect of life, Jesus has called us with a resounding, "Give!"

- Give in the physical realm of your material resource.

- Give, and open the pipeline of spiritual possibilities from the Father's reservoir.

- Give, and all things will begin to flow toward you so they might abound through you — in *all* your life — materially, physically and spiritually.

He concludes this call with an overwhelming declaration of intended abundance.

Jesus' Overflowing

Finally, describing the abundance He'll bring to our lives, Jesus uses an agricultural symbol. It's one that would have been instantly understood in that ancient culture.

It will be given to you: good measure, pressed down, shaken together, and running over (Luke 6:38).

The words *pressed down* were used in that day to describe the pressing of olives to extract the oil. In other words, those listening to our Lord would have understood Him to say, "God is going to press out all the abundance He can — for you!" And let's not miss a possibly intended second point: Jesus' figure of speech not only promises a resource of supply, but the oil being "pressed out" may well represent God's anointing — His glory flowing over our lives!

I'll say, "Amen," to that possibility: my giving in *His* spirit of release may well be the Key to a new release of His Spirit through me!

Further, Jesus uses the picture of grain being "shaken down."

We've all done that — shaken a cup of flour or a bowl of cereal to get more in. Have you noticed how you can "always" get in just a little bit more, and finally it's full? This is how Jesus encourages us. He says, "After it's reached the limit — when it's as full as it can get — I'm going to see that it runs over like grain at the time of a bumper crop!" And here again, the metaphor in the verb Jesus uses allows for expanding our expectation beyond resource or material blessing. The verb's figure of *grain* incorporates the idea of *harvest* — of souls being saved, of lives being changed! And if our Lord intends us to see the dual dimensions of His praise — material *and* spiritual blessing — then once more we are presented with an additional illustration of this giant truth: *Giving is the Key to Everything!*

So let's open up and let Him flow all of life toward us as we learn to give. And to do so, there's a starting place. Let me tell you what it is.

EIGHT

THE
STARTING
PLACE

*I don't believe for
one minute that tithing
buys God's blessing.
But I do believe that it
opens a door — or better,
a "window" — of release
for God to bless continually
and mightily.*

C OME AND sit with me at a dining-room table in San Luis Obispo. It's years ago: I'm about to turn five years old, and my parents have seated me here to introduce something that will affect my future more than I would have been able to imagine. They're both radiating the kind of happiness you'd expect when parents know they're escorting their child into a new time in his life.

As I'm seated, my dad brings out a small handful of change. Young Jack Hayford — man of the world — is about to receive two things: 1) his first allowance and 2) his first lesson in money management.

I can still remember it well.

What was true at age five would be true for years to come.

To earn my allowance, certain daily chores and weekly responsibilities around the house framed my agenda. But this memorable moment was "Payday #1." Daddy sat beside me, with Mama across the table. Because of the lesson he was ready to teach, instead of giving me a dime, he put a nickle and five pennies in front of me.

It's hard to describe the good feeling I remember. Nothing was heavy, oppressive or suffocatingly religious about what followed. The lesson was clear and concise as my dad taught me what the Bible says about tithing. I learned that day

- that tithe means "a tenth" (Gen. 28:22),

- that the Lord claims the tithe as His (Lev. 27:30),

- that obedience in tithing carries a promise (Mal. 3:10).

He explained it in such a way that it became clear to a little boy. Then, almost like a happy game, and with the healthy attitude of obedience and joy that characterized the way my folks talked about God, Daddy said, "Now, Son, from what I have just shown you, what part of this ten cents is the Lord's?"

I took a penny and answered, "This is the Lord's."

"That's right, Son," he replied. "Now, what do you want to do with it?"

"I can give it when it's offering time at Sunday school."

As they smiled their approval, Mama added, "Jack, this isn't just for today. This is for always, so you remember that. This is the way we live as a family, and we want you to learn to live that way, too. OK?"

And I said, "OK, Mama."

And I have, and I do.

As a result of parental teaching and provable evidence of God's blessing on this practice of obedience to His Word, there's not a dime or a dollar I have received in my life that I haven't tithed on.

"Still Only a Penny"

Years later, after Anna and I were married, we were approaching our first Christmas together. While finishing our college education, we were both working at the same business establishment in Los Angeles.

Each year the Christmas bonus was an entire month's salary, given in addition to our regular paychecks. It was, of course, a very marvelous and generous gift, and this year, as we received our combined gifts, we suddenly became one thousand dollars richer!

I remember sitting at the kitchen table with all of that money, getting ready to pay our bills. As we computed our tithe, for the first time in my life I was stopped in my tracks — hesitating to write the check. As I sat at the table, on the brink of writing a three-digit check of giving to the Lord for the first time, a funny thing happened to me.

Something choked inside me.

As I prepared to write the check, it suddenly seemed like such a large amount of money! I winced, feeling guilty for the possessiveness that was seeking a place in my heart. But it didn't survive for long, because almost as soon as the thought tempted me, the Lord spoke, "Child, it's still only a penny on every dime!"

I laughed, both *to* and *at* myself.

"Amen, Lord. The 'huge' tithe check isn't any more than that first penny on my first allowance!"

It's in the context of incidents like these that I have learned a pattern of tithing that has brought blessing to my whole life. I want to share this truth — freely, boldly — and for that reason.

Blessing

Now I don't believe for one minute that tithing *buys* God's blessing. But I do believe that it opens a door — or better, a "window" — of *release* for God to bless continually and mightily. The concept underlying this practice and promise is found throughout the Bible, but in the book of Malachi, God most pointedly deals with tithing. There He faces His people with the charge of neglect in the "covenant" practice.

"For I am the Lord, I do not change;
Therefore you are not consumed, O sons of Jacob.
Yet from the days of your fathers
You have gone away from My ordinances
And have not kept them.
Return to Me, and I will return to you,"
Says the Lord of hosts.
"But you said,
'In what way shall we return?'

"Will a man rob God?
Yet you have robbed Me!
But you say, 'In what way have we robbed You?'
In tithes and offerings.
You are cursed with a curse,
For you have robbed Me,
Even this whole nation.
Bring all the tithes into the storehouse,
That there may be food in My house,
And try Me now in this,"
Says the Lord of hosts,
"If I will not open for you the windows of heaven
And pour out for you such blessing
That there will not be room enough to receive it.

"And I will rebuke the devourer for your sakes,
So that he will not destroy the fruit of your
  ground,
Nor shall the vine fail to bear fruit for you in the
  field,"
Says the Lord of hosts;
"And all nations will call you blessed,
For you will be a delightful land,"
Says the Lord of hosts (Mal. 3:6-12).

In this passage, the Lord calls for the return of His people. But when they ask, "In what way shall we return?" (v. 7), the Lord says something completely foreign to our way of thinking.

- He doesn't tell them to get on their knees and pray.

- He doesn't instruct them to read the Bible

- He doesn't demand they go to the temple more often.

Rather, He starts by talking to them about their money — about tithing. Notice that it's His starting place.

First, the Lord contrasts His own changelessness with the *un*faithfulness of their fathers. That reference takes us back to the fall of man, where humankind first became broken and afflicted through the fall of our common father, Adam. It's that fallenness which stands in stark contrast to God's unchanging holiness. It's what lies at the root of our fears, our being so ingrained with a grasping desire for selfish control of our lives and the fearful reticence to give. It all flows to us from that fall.

Though God created us and promised to sustain us, it is a great difficulty for many of us to give God His portion. It's important to see our human resistance to tithing as another expression of our fallen nature. Consider the following perspective on the first sin.

God's Portion

Before the fall of man, God gave Adam and his wife stewardship over *all creation*.

> So God created man in His own image; in the image of God He created him; male and female He created them. Then God blessed them, and God said to them, "Be fruitful and multiply; fill the earth and subdue it; have dominion over the fish of the sea, over the birds of the air, and over every living thing that moves on the earth" (Gen. 1:27-28).

After this, God said, in effect, "I only ask one thing of you: that you honor the fact that a certain portion of creation is Mine and Mine alone." That's essentially what God said when He told Adam not to eat of the tree of the knowledge of good and evil (Gen. 2:16-17).

We usually think of that prohibition as only being "to eat or not to eat." But the issue was deeper. It was an issue of *recognized rights*. It involved man understanding and accepting that a small portion of all he had within his reach was reserved — it belonged to the Lord. The Lord said, "Everything else is yours, but this is Mine."

We are dealing with exactly the same issue when we discuss the tithe — God's claim on 10 percent of our income. And that's why I call tithing "the starting place" for our learning to give — because it relates so directly to our knowing and honoring the difference between what is God's and what is ours.

> And all the tithe of the land, whether of the seed of the land or of the fruit of the tree, is the Lord's. It is holy to the Lord (Lev. 27:30).

Of course, we know so well the events at the beginning.

Satan came, tempting the man and woman and saying, in effect, "God knows that if you ever get hold of His portion, too, you'll be so much better off than you are now" (see Gen. 3:5).

How easily we're persuaded by the supposition that if we can just have what God says is His, we'll be better off! And the tempter succeeded, with the bottom line being that man tried to take God's job into his own hands.

"You will be like God," the serpent hissed, and man fell for it. The tragedy is that all of God's likeness that they needed was already theirs, for God had created them marvelously and miraculously, fully in His image (see Gen. 1:26). They didn't need God's *power*, only the blessing of His *Person* imprinted in their nature. They didn't need God's *position*, only the *promise* of His provision to sustain their every need. But in Adam and Eve's pursuit of "acquiring," they took God's portion, thereby not only losing what they thought they would gain, but what they already had as well.

The analogy to our human temptation, to take the tithe which is the Lord's and to administrate it as our own, is an essential perspective. To see the divine claim on 10 percent of our income and to surrender it in worship, faithfully, is to find life's financial starting place and life's essential beginning point of blessing once we're in Christ.

His Pattern and Blueprint

All of us understand the concept of a pattern or blueprint. The tailor who designed the clothes you're wearing had to follow a pattern or the clothing would not fit. It would be too tight in some places, or it would be too loose and would feel uncomfortable in other places if it were not made according to pattern. A building would not be safe, nor would an engine run, if not made according to the blueprint.

It is the same thing with life. We have to start right.

The Bible's patterns for life are not merely *religious* rules, they're *right* rules. That is, they're *patterns that work* so we can live life the way God designed it. His commandments and precepts are blueprints — designs provided so we can build lives that stand strong and tall. Meanwhile, we can wear life like a comfortably fitting suit — living in the likeness and blessing of God's purposes which are working for our benefit and for His glory.

The pattern for godliness that God gave Adam included directions on how mankind is to relate to any portion that God says is His. And since the Bible says we are to begin relating to our money by rendering the tithe as the Lord's, we're wise to do so, remembering always that God is a giving God, not a taker. And He wants to make us in His image as a giving people. By starting with the tithe, He creates for us an opportunity to see what He can do to make us *like Him* — that's what godly or Christlike really means.

As we honor God with our tithes, we are beginning at a place which, if you will, starts "unbending" the key which was bent when man fell: the Key to Everything. So, opening with our new birth in Christ and continuing with our willingness to submit to God's order, we're called forward in life. And becoming willing to worship Him with our tithes is a "key" step in seeing life's Key begin to straighten out. When we link practical obedience in giving with our potential for growth in living, we're en route to seeing all of life start to fit — to open up again.

Rob God? How?

Malachi's message pointed back to the beginning — "your fathers." And so we've seen how *early* the issue of man taking God's portion became a problem. Then the prophet asks a strange question: "Will a man rob God?" (Mal. 3:8).

What can this mean?

It's important here to say the obvious: God *doesn't* have a cash-flow problem! So how is it that the prophet says that the people's not tithing had "robbed" Him? A look at the whole text answers the question: *God had been robbed of His opportunity to bless His people!*

That's His heart — His desire. God wants to bless! Notice that when He says that if we'll return, He'll open the windows of heaven and pour out a blessing we won't be able to contain, the Lord isn't merely talking about financial benefit. He's talking about *all* His blessings. The "windows of heaven" aren't a bank, but they are the openings from which *all* life's benedictions flow.

- When the windows of heaven are open over your home, there is joy and happiness.

- When the windows of heaven are open over your business, there is fruitfulness and prosperity.

- When the windows of heaven are open over your mind, there is peace and confidence.

- When the windows of heaven are open over your body and soul, there is health and contentment.

"The windows of heaven" are the Bible's words to describe the source from which God blesses, and that's what God delights to bring about. That's what the generosity of His love *doesn't* want to be "robbed" of expressing! So God's request for our tithe isn't an appeal from a hard-pressed deity suffering for cash. It's a request that we not deprive Him of blessing us in very real ways. He's calling us to order our finances on the earth side of things in a way that lines up with the release of special graces waiting to be poured out from the heaven side of things. Tithing starts right — by aligning us under the place where the blessings of God are released: heaven's windows.

But the decision to tithe is ours.

Just as surely as the Lord Jesus Christ knocks at the doors

of our hearts and says, "If you'll open the door, I'll come in, and you'll be saved," we have that choice. And having received Him as Savior, we can stop there or move ahead as His disciples. The wisest and most sensitive of us choose growing in Him, making Him Lord in our life's daily matters. And nothing says, "Yes, Lord," any clearer than our obedience and our worship with our tithe.

Let me say it again. Neither God nor I am making a legal demand, declaring that if you don't tithe, you're not going to heaven. Salvation transcends legalistic demands. But I am dealing with a principle of giving which God has wrapped into the very structure of creation. The law of gravity manifests predictable responses in the created universe. So does giving. When I *let go*, when I *give*, when I *release*, I make room for life and abundance to flow into my life according to God's order.

When I line up at "the starting place" of tithing, I gain victory over my human vulnerability to a subtle form of incipient idolatry which asks: "Will I put my faith in God's management principles or in my own management skill?"

If I hesitate to start tithing because I'm worried about how I'm going to make it, and in my effort to make ends meet I violate the Lord's first principle of giving, am I succumbing to a deception luring me to put myself in God's place? Am I saying that I am better able to make things work out than God is?

Loved one, having chosen to put our faith in Jesus, let's proceed to know *all* the life He has for us. Unbending the key of tithing is one of the most powerful decisions we can make. It's a crucial starting place in moving toward the full realization for God's highest plans for all our lives.

It's true.

But some still insist otherwise.

NINE

A TIRED
QUESTION

*By the affirmation
of Jesus our Lord Himself,
tithing is thereby
made a timeless
practice, as important
to New Testament
believers as to Old.*

EVEN THOUGH the Bible clearly reveals tithing as a divinely ordered, financial discipline with the wonderful promises attending and guaranteed by God Himself, some still raise a tired question: "Isn't tithing only in the Old Testament?"

The idea in this expressed doubt is that tithing is part of the law and therefore has no meaning to New Testament believers. This resistance usually projects the notion that teaching tithing will deprive a Christian of his "liberty" or move a believer "into law and out of grace."

But the truth of the tithe is not only in the Old Testament. The New Testament shows tithing as appropriate for us today as for believers during *all* history. God's Word also reveals that *all* His blessings and covenants are of grace, not law.

Jesus Himself addressed the issue of tithing. It's recorded in two New Testament books — Matthew and Luke.

Jesus was dealing with the Pharisees — a tough breed of religionists who were looking for every way they could to attend to the letter of the law without attending to its spiritual demands. As we noted earlier, Jesus observed that they tithed, but He had attacked their supposition that obedience to a "ritual" released them from the larger reality of obedience to love's responsibilities. Let's look again at Jesus' exact words.

> Woe to you, scribes and Pharisees, hypocrites! For you pay tithe of mint and anise and cummin, and have neglected the weightier matters of the law: justice and mercy and faith. These you ought to have done, without leaving the others undone (Matt. 23:23; see also Luke 11:42).

Now look closely with me so we make no mistake about what is and what isn't said.

The "woe" on these religious hypocrites was *not* for their tithing, but for their neglect of "weightier matters" — justice, mercy and faith. Now, the Pharisees were attending to the letter of the law in the presenting of their tithes, and it wasn't just a matter of bringing one bushel of wheat out of every ten. They were even weighing out the tithe of the tiniest spices — mint and cummin!

Think now.

If tithing was unimportant to the Savior, if it was meaningless to maintain within the new order He was bringing, then as a part of emphasizing that new order He could well have said, "Take care of justice and mercy, and quit bothering with tithing — mint, cummin or anything else!" But instead Jesus says, "These you ought to have done" — referring to their *tithing* — "without leaving the others undone" — referring to their *attitudes*.

In affirming their practice of tithing, Jesus employs what grammarians call "the moral imperative." He uses the word *ought*. When we acknowledge that something ought to be, we are appealing to a higher order — to the divine will. We are saying, "There are certain laws that should not be violated." Thus, with His "ought," Jesus is saying of the practice of tithing, "This is a precept that ought not to be violated." By the affirmation of Jesus our Lord Himself, tithing is thereby made a *timeless* practice, as important to New Testament believers as to Old.

Tithing as a New Testament practice is even further verified in the book of Romans. We are specifically admonished to walk "in the steps of faith which our father Abraham" walked (Rom. 4:12). This isn't the only place the New Testament notes Abraham as a pattern of faith for us to follow today. What Abraham experienced is an example for us. It is relevant not only because he manifested a faith that walked "seeing the invisible" (Heb. 11:1), but also because he was one to whom the Lord gave covenant promises (Heb. 11:13), promises which parallel our lives today.

In tracing the footsteps of Abraham, we find that Scripture says of him: "And he gave him [Melchizedek] a tithe of all" (Gen. 14:20). Abraham is revealed as a man who learned the pathway to promise before the law was ever given! See it, loved one? Tithing was established in the Scripture *before* the law of Moses. It precedes and transcends the Mosaic code as a principle built into the fabric of the human order of things.

Tithing may have begun in the Old Testament, but its spirit, truth and practice proceed unto today. God's Word underscores it as ours to believe, rejoice in, worship with and be rewarded by!

There's yet another New Testament lesson here. See the spirit — the heart and the wisdom — of Abraham in the *way* he worshipped with his tithes.

Hebrews 7 (certainly New Testament!) notes how Abraham brought tithes to Melchizedek, who is a biblical type of our

Lord Jesus Christ. When Abraham brought his tithe, his action was one of worship to God: "I have raised my hand to the Lord, God Most High, the Possessor of heaven and earth" (Gen. 14:22). There's a holy completeness to this declaration. This man was saying what understanding, worshipping tithers say to this day: "In this act, I'm saying that I'm surrendered and devoted to the God of all creation!"

Then, see how Melchizedek, the priest of the Lord, responded. He spoke the blessing of God on Abraham: "Blessed be Abram of the God Most High, Possessor of heaven and earth" (v. 19). Both the words of the priest and the worshipper make a declaration about God: He is the Almighty — the Source of all things. Ultimately and conclusively, all things are *from* Him and *to* Him. The whole world is in His hands, so everything I possess I have from the Lord, and in my worship I acknowledge this with my tithe.

The ultimate reality concerning all life and all resources is that they not only *come* from God, but *belong* to Him as well. Abraham understood that, and he charted a pathway of walking in that faith — and he walked that path as a tither.

- The New Testament calls us to walk in Abraham's footsteps.

- Jesus says tithing is an "ought to."

- The idea of the tithe being the Lord's cannot be confined to Old Testament teaching.

Having seen how God's Word firmly ensconces tithing as a privilege and practice appropriate under the new covenant as well as the old, return with me to look at what follows in God's promise through Malachi. There's an "overcoming" feature within tithing, too!

Rebuking the Devourer

To cap off the grand truth of the tithe, God makes an incredible promise. As a part of His response to our worshipping Him through the faith-exercise of tithes and offerings, He says, "I will rebuke the devourer for your sakes" (Mal. 3:11). It's another evidence of the fact that how we deal with our money is a spiritual issue touching all of life. These words reveal that when we obey in the material realm, it impacts the spiritual realm, too.

Who is "the devourer"?

Jesus taught us that we have a common enemy whose animosity is leveled toward all mankind. The Word shows him especially hateful toward people who seek to honor God in any area of their lives.

> The thief does not come except to steal, and to kill, and to destroy. I have come that they may have life, and that they may have it more abundantly (John 10:10).

> Be sober, be vigilant; because your adversary the devil walks about like a roaring lion, seeking whom he may devour (1 Pet. 5:8).

The thief advances with viciousness and, in terms of our finances, devours in some of the most obvious ways. Breakdowns. Repairs needed. An unexplainable onslaught of illness. The dishwasher or the garbage disposal goes "pop," and there goes $79.50 out the window or $123.52 down the drain. Investments go sour. Money owed us isn't paid. The devourer often comes in any or all such things that eat up — or devour — our resources.

Now God doesn't promise that we'll never have a car breakdown or that mechanical things will never wear out if we tithe. Neither is tithing a formula guarantee that we'll never have to get flu shots. But the Lord does say, "These things aren't going to eat you up!"

As we learn the liberty of full, free, let-go obedience to the Lord and His ways, we have an overcoming promise. God says He will make it His mission to rebuke the oppressive forces that chew up our finances and cause reversal in our situations. He means He will speak His Word of power against the adversary. He means that as we attend to our ministry of worship-filled giving to Him, He will oversee our times of trial and not be silent. Tithing holds no magic promise of trial-free living, but tithing does have a share in the promise that when we face trials of any kind, we have reason to expect God to come against the advances of our adversary.

The Windows of Blessing

Now let's summarize:

1. God's ability to "renew" His purpose in our lives is dependent upon our coming to Christ, and by that act, salvation's covenant is established.

2. God's capacity to "fulfill" His purpose in us is dependent upon our obedience to the principles of His creative order.

3. Many people are saved for *eternity* but fail to allow more of God's gracious power and purposes to flow into their lives in this *time*.

4. With regard to our giving, the Lord has said that to neglect tithing "robs" Him of His high joy at seeing His benevolent intent fulfilled in us. He says He's been "robbed" of the chance to bless us. Then He adds a new concept: The absence of His blessing allows the presence of a "curse" to rule instead. What is this about?

Cursed?

The "curse" is what we are all exposed to as mε
fallen race — creatures on a broken planet. It isn
lated action of a retaliatory deity. But sin's curse ε   ˌᴜes
today as the sad by-product of sin, impacting any life lived
outside the umbrella of redemption's promise.

Now when God says, "You are cursed with a curse" (Mal.
3:9), some conjure the image of God as something of a
heavenly warlock, bent intently over an enormous pot of evil
brew, which He's readying for any chance He may get to
pour over people who offend Him. The unspoken notion of
many is that God is "almost hoping" people will disobey Him
so He can justly "lay a good curse" on them.

But this idea is nowhere near the true biblical picture of
our Creator. To the contrary, He's a God of blessing, not
cursing. And through Jesus' death, He has made a way for us
to live out from under the cursed order of things.

In Christ we have been redeemed from the curse (Gal.
3:13). As we live in His Word, we can find a place under the
"umbrella" of grace — a place where life begins to function
the right way again. Joy will flow. Adequacy is found.

But if we depart from the Lord's ways or neglect His
life-nourishing principles, His promises of intended blessing
turn inside out. They become curses to us, as the perversion
of our disobedience inverts His Word. The reverse of that
Word becomes the opposite of blessing, not because *He*
changed but because *we* turned from following His ways.
God doesn't want to see curses come on anybody. That's
why He said to the people, "Return to Me" (Mal. 3:7). He is
a God of salvation and not destruction!

Still, there is a devourer seeking to curse, to swallow up,
to eat through and spit out, if you please. And whether we
like it or not, choosing not to tithe is to choose to step out
from under God's umbrella of blessing. Without His protec-
tion, you and I are far more vulnerable to life's "rain" of

ircumstance — however mild or fierce. The choice is ours.

So the Lord calls us to "prove Him," to give Him the opportunity to pour out blessings on us that we cannot contain. He says that He will open the windows of heaven and rebuke the devourer (vv. 10-11). The first is a promise of abundance, and the other is a promise of victory over the adversary. These promises directly relate to the starting place for my giving — my tithe. I think that, more than we know, tithing may be God's appointed starting place from which we learn the *supernatural* dimensions of His power in the material realm as well as the spiritual. Let me share with you a brief article I recently wrote for my congregation.

Money and the Miraculous

A fellow pastor told me a peculiar story the other day. One of his members asked to be removed from membership since tithing was one of the church's requirements for being a member. Because we have that requirement (following other more eternal issues, of course, such as salvation and water baptism), I listened all the more closely. The man said he still wanted to attend the church "because," he said, "I like the teaching — I just don't believe in tithing anymore."

Aside from being bewildered by the incongruity of such posturing ("I believe what you teach except when I don't believe it," a position of supposed "discernment" I guess), I started thinking about the broader issue of tithing as taught in God's eternal Word. Suddenly I was impacted with a fresh perspective on the *miraculous* nature of this truth.

Having practiced and taught tithing most of my life, I was amazed I hadn't seen this dimension of giving with this intensity before. It struck me that, just like our faith in the invisible God, tithing is a statement of commitment to acknowledge the power of the Creator. When I voluntarily give at least 10 percent of my budget into His kingdom enterprise, I'm saying, "I can '*see*' His ability to create enough to make my budget run with less than the unbeliever claims he needs."

In addition to hearing the story the pastor told me, I've faced a flurry of questions from people who've recently heard a series presented by two different Christian radio broadcasters, both rejecting the New Testament teaching on tithing. Oddly enough (or is it?), *both* the broadcasters are men who oppose the present supernatural works of the Holy Spirit in the church; that is, gifts, signs and wonders. I bear neither any ill will, but on considering this, I realized something I find significant: I cannot remember ever hearing a person oppose tithing who was committed to faith in the present stream of the Holy Spirit's miraculous works!

This marvelous age of God's gracious dealing through the church is focused in one word — *promise* — and all in one name — *Jesus*. The old saw that "tithing is Old Testament" has had its teeth removed by our Lord Himself. He reinforced tithing and brought it to the level of "ought to" (Matt. 23:23; Luke 11:42) — the moral imperative — while also commending bold, believing generosity in giving (Luke 6:38). When we couple Jesus' words with Paul's expositon of how the "glory" of the New Testament life excelled any practice or principle in the Mosaic law (see 2 Cor. 3:7-8), we see the tithing question is answered rather conclusively for anyone knowing that believers are people of "the promise" (see Acts 2:38-39; Gal. 3:29).

In short, it becomes inconceivable that a person moving in New Testament faith would *retreat* to anything less than Old Testament standards. Whether those are standards of holy living or holy giving, the issue is not that we obey to *earn* God's favor; rather, that we have *learned* to abound in the resources of His promises and in the Holy Spirit's power to make them work in our lives!

To tithe isn't to submit to a *legal code* but to become open to the *regal conduct* of kingdom people. It's a realm of faith that lifts us beyond the limits of fear and doubt and into trust and obedience. We learn to walk like Peter did; who, upon hearing Jesus say, "Come unto me," walked on water. Similarly, we "see" the Word of promise underwritten by His power, and — with regard to tithing as well as in other areas of life — we walk with heaven's eyesight (by faith) and not from earth's viewpoint (by sight). (See 2 Cor. 5:7.)

Let me suggest that, if you want to bridge the gulf of your financial situation, don't attempt to build with ten planks of your own resources. Instead, put one of the planks in God's hands and then lay the others. And when you arrive at that place where you thought there wouldn't be a plank to step on while crossing the chasm, you'll find out that you don't fall. You'll make it *all* the way, and you'll also find incredible blessing on the other side (Mal. 3:10-12)! It's all a part of dealing with God's promise in the realm of money and the miraculous.

Those words to my flock were a reaffirmation of giving's starting place, but another principle is closely related: *the law of sowing and reaping*. It's a principle that causes confusion to some dear believers — confusion that can be dispelled. Let me point you to the enriching practice of sowing — how to plant for the future.

TEN

PLANTING FOR THE FUTURE

*Givers...are called primarily
to sow toward a harvest.
We are people whose mission,
more than anything else,
is to meet mankind's
greatest need: to know the
love of God in Jesus Christ.*

NOT LONG after the signing of the Constitution of the United States, a baby named John Chapman was born in Massachusetts. Not much is known about his early years, but we do know that early in his young manhood, John worked in a western Pennsylvania cider mill. At that time, in the early 1800s, Pennsylvania was on the western frontier of the nation. Some had started to move westward beyond that boundary, but many believed the country was too rugged and undeveloped to settle.

It was while he was working at that the cider mill that John Chapman became possessed with an idea and a vision that gripped his heart and became more influential in preparing the way for the future of a nation than he could ever have dreamed.

One obvious by-product of work at the cider mill was seeds — piles and piles of apple seeds, left over after the pressing process. They formed mounds which seemed useless to most. But one man saw their virtue, and these seeds became central to the vision which captivated John Chapman.

One day, after extensive preliminary planning, Chapman filled large bags with the seeds, quit his job and prepared to head west. As he traveled, he planted apple trees all along the way.

The young man was very clear in his purpose. Like thousands of would-be settlers, he had become gripped by a vision of a young nation's westward expansion. But John Chapman saw a different view of the challenge the West held. He knew that when increasing multitudes eventually came west to settle and establish families, little would be available to sustain them during their travels and to secure their arrival at settling sites. So all along the trails and where future farms might develop, this visionary planted seed in random places and in complete orchards. He did it in the expectation that when the pioneers would follow, fruit would be available — waiting for them.

He faced the elements, learning to interface with the Indians and meeting hardships in the pursuit of his dream. He was also a man of faith, said to be committed to the Word of God and the testimony of Jesus Christ. It's told that he not only planted seeds in the ground, but he also carried spiritual seeds that he planted in the hearts of men and women. He was a man with a vision for the future, seeing tomorrow's possibilities for a fledgling country and sowing into its future as an act of faith.

Some who debunk history have said the man was insane. But the world will probably always think that those who give their life to a vision — who plant for the future — are not worthy of society's approval. But notwithstanding the assessment some made of Chapman, others say the man was a pivotal personality in early U. S. history, like Daniel Boone or Kit Carson — one among key men who paved the way to what became a great nation.

Today a small monument has been raised to Chapman in the heartland of America. Placed in a small park in Indiana, you can visit the burial site — the tribute serious souls have given in assessment of the man's life and contribution.

But when you look for it, you'll find it under another name — the affectionate name given him nearly two centuries ago by settlers whose lives were made a little easier because of John Chapman's vision. They called him *Johnny Appleseed.*

People of Vision

There's something stirring, something stimulating about the story of Johnny Appleseed. Few can read it and not feel, "That's the kind of person I want to be!"

- A person who *sees* tomorrow

- A person who *sows* in faith

- A person who *serves* and blesses

This kind of person plants for the future. The apostle Paul was seeking to cultivate these qualities when he wrote the following:

> But I rejoiced in the Lord greatly that now at last your care for me has flourished again; though you surely did care, but you lacked opportunity. Not that I speak in regard to need, for I have learned in whatever state I am, to be content: I know how to be abased, and I know how to abound. Everywhere and in all things I have learned both to be full and

to be hungry, both to abound and to suffer need. I can do all things through Christ who strengthens me.

Nevertheless you have done well that you shared in my distress. Now you Philippians know also that in the beginning of the gospel, when I departed from Macedonia, no church shared with me concerning giving and receiving but you only. For even in Thessalonica you sent aid once and again for my necessities. Not that I seek the gift, but I seek the fruit that abounds to your account. Indeed I have all and abound. I am full, having received from Epaphroditus the things sent from you, a sweet-smelling aroma, an acceptable sacrifice, well pleasing to God (Phil. 4:10-18).

Paul's choice of terminology is taken directly from the sacrificial system of the Old Testament. The words *sweet-smelling aroma* and *acceptable sacrifice* recall the ancient peace offering brought simply to thank God for the peace of heart and mind enjoyed in knowing Him.

Epaphroditus' personal sacrifice and service reflected this spirit (Phil. 2:25-30). So did the unselfish giving of the Philippians themselves (Phil. 4:10-18). Further yet, the same spirit is designated in Paul's own dedication to the epistle (Phil. 1:20-21; 2:17). All in all, this epistle, its primary addressees as well as the bearer and the writer of the letter, characterizes the order of "people who give."

Here are New Testament people who give, *not only* out of joy and a sense of relationship with the Lord, *but also* by reason of their recognition of a unique opportunity into which they may pour themselves. They do so 1) in anticipation of future fruitfulness and 2) when they recognize a God-given opportunity.

Notice how Paul seems to say, "You've not given for some time, Philippians, but I know it wasn't because you didn't care. It was simply that *you didn't have the opportunity*" (see Phil. 4:10).

Capture that concept! It's the key to the principle of *sowing* — of planting for the future. It's the action taken by people who recognize an opportunity for effective advancement of the gospel and "sow a seed" into it.

Sowing in Faith

This agricultural image of "sowing in faith" is as old as history itself. Over the last several years it has become an increasingly used term among believers in Christ. My personal feeling is that the Holy Spirit is employing this principle to awaken the church with an eye toward advancing ministry dramatically and dynamically as we move toward the last days' harvest.

In the term *last days' harvest*, we incorporate a combination of convictions:

- That Jesus Christ is coming soon, and we anticipate His return

- That the world is in desperate need, and there are souls we want to reach

- That the advance of the gospel requires the investment of dedicated believers who care

- That the call to give freely does not remove the obvious fact that people still have their own personal needs and can't give everything they have

The last observation is fundamental to this chapter. I'm wondering if you've ever asked yourself this question: "Though I may want to give, I do not have a great deal to give Where do I derive the faith to give out of my limited resources in order to advance what I see as a great opportunity for the gospel?"

I believe the answer to this question is in Scripture, in the examples of the "sowing" kind of faith shown by people like the the church at Philippi. There are examples all throughout the New Testament.

Turn with me to another letter from Paul and see the precise terminology being applied to people who had *very* limited resources and yet gave with *great* faith.

> Moreover, brethren, we make known to you the grace of God bestowed on the churches of Macedonia: that in a great trial of affliction the abundance of their joy and their deep poverty abounded in the riches of their liberality. For I bear witness that according to their ability, yes, and beyond their ability, they were freely willing, imploring us with much urgency that we would receive the gift and the fellowship of the ministering to the saints (2 Cor. 8:1-4).

The setting which attends this majestic demonstration of faith-inspired giving is one that is explained by ancient historians. At this time a great drought had taken hold throughout the Roman Empire. It was having a severe economic impact on many of the major areas of commerce. Here Paul, writing to the Corinthians to invite their visionary giving, makes reference to their fellow Christians who lived in the northern part of ancient Greece — the region of Macedonia.

The specific wording in the text seems so contradictory by human analysis! The apostle describes people giving out of *deep poverty*, with the results being *riches*. What is Paul saying?

First, we are reading about people who had a motivation birthed in an understanding of God's natural laws. They apparently realized that God's laws are as real in the material realm as they are in the agricultural realm. Their spiritual giving and sacrifice — beyond their actual capacity to give — was born from their grasp of the principle of sowing and reaping.

> Now may He who supplies seed to the sower, and bread for food, supply and multiply the seed you have sown and increase the fruits of your righteousness, while you are enriched in everything for all liberality which causes thanksgiving through us to God (2 Cor. 9:10-11).

Paul exhorts the Corinthians to capture that understanding which had already moved the Macedonians to action. They saw clearly that when they gave, the same principle operated in the *financial* realm that God had established in the *farming* realm. Just as a farmer depended upon the blessing the Creator had put on his "invested seed," the same Creator took the financial "seed" invested when a person gave — no matter how little — and *He multiplied it.*

Today, as in Paul's time, "seed faith" is best focused on the larger purpose of the harvest of souls around the world. The objective moving the Macedonians was *others*, not themselves.

Such giving should never be entered as the result of human manipulation. It ought to be born of vision and faith. Neither should seed-faith giving ever be motivated by an unholy sense of guilt or obligation. That's why the apostle Paul emphasizes in 2 Corinthians 9:7:

> So let each one give as he purposes in his heart, not grudgingly or of necessity; for God loves a cheerful giver.

This same text sets the tone for that order of faith-inspired giving that goes beyond what natural man would give. That tone is in the words of one of the most quoted sentences in the Bible: "God loves a cheerful giver." The words deserve to be restated again and again so the following fact may be understood: If your giving is born of fear, guilt or pressure, it's not born of God's Spirit.

This needs to be learned by dear saints who are sometimes so fearful of displeasing God that they take faithless action in the name of "faith." It *can* result in deadly frustration.

This issue has become very important to me as a pastor, for often I will have parishoners ask if they have disobeyed God by not responding to an appeal from a ministry that asked them to "sow in faith." My answer is always the same. If faith isn't ignited in your heart when you hear of the need, and if your soul doesn't rejoice at the prospect of sowing that seed, then God isn't telling you to give. You aren't being disobedient.

You see, the very evidence that we are being called to take a specific action of sowing in *faith* carries with it the companion promise that the Holy Spirit does and will stir that faith *with joy* when it's *He* calling you to action. Then the whole experience will be one of genuine worship and rejoicing.

Let me tell you a couple of stories to illustrate this.

Sowing Ourselves

Remember my mention of Johnny Appleseed's grave?

I discovered his gravesite at a time in my life when Anna and I were sowing seed — *ourselves*. It was a challenging and demanding time in the life of our young family, but it was always joy-filled. We were blessed and happy all the time, even though need always seemed to be present!

For example, on any given Tuesday during those years in our early pastoral experience, you could have gone to the local government agency providing surplus food commodities for the poor and seen Pastor Jack Hayford in line along with other limited-income people in the community.

I remember those days with a smile, especially because in my days of training for pastoral ministry, I'd been told, "A pastor *always* is to be dressed in suit and tie when in public." So each Tuesday, I'd join the line of poor people, fully qualified to receive the government's surplus by reason of an almost non-existent salary, yet dressed for Sunday church! I looked like a freeloader, lying about his income to get food "on the dole."

It's a humorous image, but let me tell you: I can't get the same quality of food today no matter how much I spend! We received the finest cheese, butter, cornmeal, flour and powdered milk from the heartland of America's finest farms. It was not to be surpassed by anything sold in the local grocery store. Oh, to be *that* "poor" again!

Although our resources were limited as we pursued our call, we were happy. Why? Because we were serving an *opportunity* — an opportunity to sow ourselves into the work of God's kingdom. And our sowing of ourselves did bring a harvest — an ingathering of scores of people who came to Jesus as their Savior during those few years of diligent effort. There were homes rescued from confusion, young people aimed on a course of Christian faithfulness, and human souls born into eternal life.

We still receive letters these many years later from the dear people we were allowed to serve in those early days that seem so distant now. They remind us of the truth that sowing in faith reaps a harvest in two places: 1) in the *spiritual* realm where vision reaches and 2) in the *material* realm where need is met.

My second story occurred almost twenty years later.

I was driving home from north Los Angeles County where I had been conducting a weekly Bible study for several months. A group of people who had visited our church in Van Nuys asked if I would come and hold meetings with the possibility a new church could be born in their area. Our family had limited income then, even though we wouldn't qualify as "poverty level" anymore. But with four children — two ready to enter college — and with the extra expense of making a hundred-mile round trip each week to plant this new church, our family budget was stretched.

I have never made a fee a requirement in any situation in which I have ministered, so in going to these meetings I'd made no stipulations. However, the people would periodically receive a love offering for me. So it was that following one of those occasions I was driving home one night with $168 in currency and change that had been given to me that evening.

As I drove, I was computing what I was going to do with the money. Of course, seventeen dollars was tithe. Then, too, Anna and I have always given offerings beyond our tithe, so I made a decision in that regard. I also deducted the cost of a few minor bills we had at home and, having finished these mental computations, I had an experience I had never had yet in my life.

I was over forty years of age and had *never* had the experience of having *extra* money.

I couldn't believe it!

I was driving home, and suddenly I became aware of a startling fact — I had almost one hundred dollars with nothing I actually had to spend it on! It seemed almost a miracle with its own element of excitement, thrill and praise to God! But then a funny thing happened: I started to feel guilty.

My reason for guilt was an inner feeling — never taught me but somehow "felt" — that if I ever had anything extra, I needed to give it away. Nothing in the Bible requires that. But somehow, never having had any real discretionary money in my adult life, I was unprepared to know how to deal with it.

I paused to pray.

"Lord," I asked, "what do You want me to do with this money? I know You don't want me to feel guilty, so I need

You to help me understand how to manage these resources. I've never had this experience before."

I suppose some people will think this story is either a peculiar confession or an invented one. Perhaps, on the one hand, you've always had sufficient provision; you've never been in such a position. But I'm telling it exactly as it was. Please be assured, I'm not relating this story either to sound pathetic about my life or to suggest that you should feel spoiled for having more than I had.

On the other hand, I can't help but think someone will fully identify with my experience of limited resources but might be tempted to ask the question, "Why hasn't God ever given *me* an extra hundred dollars?" I'm not indifferent to such vulnerability, with its temptation to think you might be less spiritual for not yet having had this experience. But I *don't* feel that, and your spirituality *isn't* related to the amount of money you have or haven't. But let me tell you what the Lord's answer to me was that night.

I sat there thinking, with the hum of the car's engine providing the only sound as I continued homeward. I didn't expect the clear, immediate answer God gave me.

I'd simply uttered my prayer as an expression of hope for guidance on how to think about my "sudden wealth," when moments later the Lord spoke back to me: "You have learned to be abased. Now I'm going to teach you how to abound."

It was at once a *revelation*, a *teaching* and a *comfort*.

- It was a *revelation* because the Holy Spirit gave me an immediate insight.

- It was a *teaching* because I saw practical steps that I could take.

- It was a *comfort* because I was relieved of the uncertainty and guilt I had felt.

129

1. Revelation

The *revelation* had to do with the concept of "abasing and abounding," words Paul used in speaking to the Philippians.

> Not that I speak in regard to need, for I have learned in whatever state I am, to be content: I know how to be abased, and I know how to abound. Everywhere and in all things I have learned both to be full and to be hungry, both to abound and to suffer need. I can do all things through Christ who strengthens me (Phil. 4:11-13).

I had always thought of "abasing" as a humiliating punishment, something which might be inflicted on a person as a judgment or an embarrassment. Even though I'd read those words in Scripture before, my interpretation had been that Paul's learning to be "abased" referred to such times as his being assaulted, beaten, shipwrecked, etc. But the context actually points to times of financial restrictions (see vv. 10-18), and he says that in these times of deficiency he had "learned...to be content."

Clearly, then, abasing wasn't a season of whimpering by a man who sees himself suffering and is complaining about it. It's simply a term related to the facts of a person's financial limitations, much like those first two decades of our marriage and family life. We never felt deprived. And God always met our needs. But extras were rarely known, except sometimes on holiday occasions when special gifts were received.

How many people experience this very same thing in the early years of their lives or marriages — limited income by reason of being new in their professions, trying to pay off educational debts, financing beginning a family and taking children through their first years of life? The same can happen at any juncture in life — unexpected turns of circumstances, job transitions, tax rate increases, lost benefits. These make up times that may well be called "abasing" —

not a punishment, not a deprivation, but simply some very real limitations.

In the same line of insight, the Lord quickened to me the concept of "abounding" — which is something He delights in. Jesus said that He came to give us life abundantly, and that it *is*, in fact, God's desire for us to know abundance. But it is also a fact that there is no promise of *perennial* abundance for any of us.

Life seesaws between times of need and times of plenty. And no believer should ever view themselves as more in the will of God at one time than another. Paul's words affirm this. "I have learned to be *both!*" And *in* both he had learned the strength of Christ to keep, sustain and supply (vv. 12-13).

2. Teaching

The Lord's very practical *teaching* touched me: "I am going to teach you to abound."

With those words I realized why I had no way of understanding how to relate to the "plenty" I suddenly had in hand. As I said, it was the first time I ever had a hundred dollars I didn't have to put on a bill or use to buy something immediately. Now the Lord was saying, as it were, "You're moving into seasons in your life when there will be cash available in ways you've not had it before. Your past would have tempted you to feel guilty or obligated to give it all away. But I am going to show you how to administrate — how to steward — resources so they can increase within your hands to serve My appointed purposes."

With this insight, I also realized intuitively that it is in God's design to allow us to simply *enjoy* having things, spending money or having a good time. This is important to realize in order to have balanced understanding. What we have is *given* by Him to serve His purpose, but it is also *within* His purpose that we may have times of simple enjoyment and plenty (see Duet. 12:20-21).

This idea offends some people.

Lingering in the collective pysche of the church of Jesus Christ is the idea of an "oath of poverty." This practice does exist. In fact, it's commendable if anyone wishes to invoke it upon himself. But it isn't required by God's Word. The oath of poverty is a church tradition, practiced by some who make this self-determination in order to pursue certain goals or ministry. It is not unlike the practice of those who choose to answer a missionary call: There's virtually *never* enough resources to answer to the demands of foreign ministry. That's one reason it merits our constant availability to *sow* into such ministry.

But in the words, "I'll teach you to *abound*," the Lord was leading me to a balance: It's OK to have a little something once in a while and enjoy it! At some times God will say, "I've given this to you to relay a gift to others," and He'll show where to sow it. At times He may say, "It's for you to enjoy." So enjoy.

3. Comfort
And His word was a comfort to me.

I not only felt comforted because the Lord was removing my temptation to feel guilty, but also comforted because God was saying He had brought me to a new time in my life during which He could trust me with new resources for financial management. It's always nice when your human father says He sees you as "growing up," and that's the way I sensed my heavenly Father felt toward me that night. So that encounter taught me certain lessons about abasing, abounding — and *abundance* — which distilled and settled into perspective. I learned

- that learning to abound doesn't mean we'll never again experience times of being abased; and that being abased refers to times of limited resources for a season, when things are in a pinch or we're going through a financial trial.

- that when we abound, it doesn't mean we've turned a corner, and now we'll be on "Easy Street" forever. Instead, abounding means God is making resources available to us so we may learn to faithfully steward them — to sow wisely.

I learned that God wants to provide a growing possibility for the ministry of financial giving to take place through us. He calls us to grow in "farmer faith," learning the principle of sowing and reaping, learning that what is true of crops is true of money — that God is the One who multiplies what is sown!

To move into this area of giving ministry, we must be sensitive to God's "appointments" for us. He will help us learn when, where and how He wants us to sow into opportunities for pioneering, for extending kingdom territory, for hastening the harvest and for planting new things. This moves us into an expanding arena of giving, beside and beyond the giving of tithes and offerings.

How will we know when to sow?

Worthy Soil

At times you will be asked to "sow" into a ministry opportunity or a needy situation. When this happens, you face the same question I do so often: Is this a ministry in which the Lord wants me to sow some resources He's given me? How can this question be answered in a spiritually sensitive way?

First, let's be comfortable with the fact that it's not only *practical* to ask the question, but the question itself is *spiritual*. I emphasize that since so many of us are moved to give when an emotional appeal deeply touches us, we may feel it *un*spiritual to even *wonder* whether we should give.

How many times have we seen television broadcasts that show the sick, the needy, the starving, the hungry, the unevangelized? At such times, *any* spiritually sensitive person would be moved. So is that my signal to give? Is the

133

existence of the *need*, in itself, a sufficient reason for me to feel constrained to send money to that ministry?

Frankly, the answer is no.

You see, dear one, need is going to be present always. Jesus said, "For you have the poor with you always, and whenever you wish you may do them good" (Mark 14:7). These are not uncompassionate words. They're Jesus' words, and He is teaching us an essential lesson.

- The poor are ever-present and important to God.

- We are to care for them, sensitively and compassionately.

- We are to do this "whenever we will"; that is, when we make a decision in the light of God's will and good sense.

Then what guidelines can help us?

Let me suggest that all sowing into ministry be made after you have asked yourself a three-part question: Is the specific ministry to which I'm thinking of giving *trustworthy*, *durable* and *committed* to the spread of the gospel?

It doesn't require the gift of discernment to realize these are important questions for us to address. Our giving ought to be directed to

- *Trustworthy ministries.* These agencies have a proven track record of fidelty and accountability. For example, today's Christian community is served by an association called the Evangelical Council on Financial Accountability (ECFA). Respected and trustworthy Christian groups will have identified with this agency or a similar one to verify their proper handling of funds. No matter how "spiritual" an individual or ministry may seem to be, you and I are responsible to make choices based on more than appearance. When sowing the seed God has put in our hands, we must be certain of the reliability of that ministry.

- *Durable ministries.* This is important not only because durability usually evidences experience in serving whatever need may be represented, but it also indicates that when the present crisis is past, the agency will still be there to follow through. This helps protect us against investing in a ministry which has a project that may seem exciting or crucial at the moment, but which spends money where no plan exists, where no strategy is present for long-term impact. The investment we make sowing into a ministry ought to have both a short-term and a continuing effect.

- *Ministries which advance the gospel of Jesus Christ.* There are many credible and meaningful non-evangelistic charitable organizations, and later I'll make clear that it *is* appropriate for Christians to give to them. But our priority should be sowing into enterprises that are promoting the gospel of Jesus Christ. Anna and I will frequently make gifts to worthy non-Christian charities. However, the preponderance of our extra-curricular giving (that is, beyond our tithes and offerings to our local church) is to Christian organizations. It's worth noting that in many instances, Christian agencies serve the same specialized realms of charity that non-Christian agencies serve. For example, there are Christian charities providing materials for the blind, for needy children, for the hungry and so forth. We always prefer to serve these special fields of human problems through gospel-oriented agencies.

In all these regards, loved one, let's remember: Givers — you and I — are called primarily to sow toward a *harvest*. We are people whose mission, more than anything else, is to meet mankind's greatest need: *to know the love of God in Jesus Christ*. We demonstrate this both by 1) witnessing the gospel of Jesus Christ to lost mankind (Matt. 28:18-20; Mark 16:15) and 2) showing the good works of charitable care to people in Jesus' name (Matt. 5:16; 25:31-46).

To learn to be a sower is to learn to enter into a new dimension of harvest. It was early in our marriage that we learned a special lesson about the blessing of sowing into God's harvest by learning the meaning of *offerings*.

Let me tell you how that happened.

ELEVEN

FREED TO "BE HUGE"

*There is too much
of a tendency to have
a poverty mentality
in today's church...
Our outlook is too small,
but that smallness
can be shaken off
in answer to our Lord
Jesus, who has called us
to be big people.*

ANNA AND I had been married only eight months when we attended our first missionary conference. If you've never been to one, let me explain.

The conference theme and messages were designed to help people capture a vision of the whole world; to see its present need for people who care and to send forth hope with the gospel of Christ's life, grace and the Father's love. There were speakers every night, films which dramatically opened our eyes to circumstances of triumph and tragedy, artifacts and representatives of different cultures. Missionaries were there from all over the world, dressed in the costumes of the areas where they served. The whole thing was colorful and stirring, heart-stretching and vision-birthing.

And the theme was a bone-cruncher: Why should anybody hear the gospel twice before everybody has heard it once?

Our hearts were touched by it all, and for very valid reasons. The world needs Jesus! And as the week drew to a close, we were asked to make "faith promises." That meant submitting commitment cards indicating how much we believed God would help us give every month for a year. The call was emphatic: "If God doesn't provide what you're 'believing for,' you have no obligation to give. But only make a commitment if you've prayed to Him about what it should be!" We were already tight in our budget, but we felt the Lord calling us to believe.

As a result, though we'd just been married, were putting ourselves through college and were facing the special budgetary demands any young couple does, Anna and I made a challenging decision. We agreed together that besides our tithe, we would give an additional 5 percent of our monthly income to missions. We agreed in prayer — asking God to help us.

Do understand, please. We weren't splitting our tithe but adding to it. We believed 1) the tithe was to be given only to the church we attended and 2) the broader need of world missions mandated our sacrifice. So we decided to believe God to help us give a total of 15 percent of our income!

Our motives were clear: We made the decision because we believed in the importance of global missions. It was significant enough to put into our budget, even though it pinched. Also, we believed that God *had* blessed us — He *blessed* us with salvation; He *blessed* us with each other; He *blessed* us with jobs and money. Further, because we knew we were called to the schooling we were pursuing, we believed He *would bless* us to see that it was paid for, too. We understood that money was a part of the Lord's blessing to us, and He would make it possible to do all that was within our budget and *still* have something left over.

That's because we also believed another thing.

We had both been giving to the Lord long enough to know that when we give, something "breaks loose." And it did.

I recall how much it thrilled us when it happened. Within a few days of that decision, changes occurred in the salary structure where we both worked, giving us *just over* five percent in salary increase — each! After we took a new step of faith and trust, the Lord gloriously provided for our new need.

What a confirmation that was to us!

Two young kids just getting started — and Jesus saying, "Let's start new things together!"

We had *not* committed beyond our salaries. We had only made a commitment that *reduced* our discretionary funds. For example, it reduced how often we could buy new clothes, what we would do for recreation or entertainment and so forth. But *now*, God had released new funds that covered our "sacrifice" and granted abundance so we could resume privileges we didn't need, but which God apparently didn't mind us enjoying!

This personal lesson was our first real schooling as a couple in applying the Bible's call to bring *both* tithes and offerings unto the Lord.

The King's Portion

As I explained earlier, tithes are not a gift to God. He "claims" them as His own (Lev. 27:30). While it is our privilege to comply with tithing and ours to present in anticipation of experiencing the joyous benefits that come from such alignment to His kingly throne, the truth is that our tithes are actually God's to begin with.

In employing the figure of "tithing to His kingly throne," I am using a metaphor consistent with ancient kingdoms in which the "throne" — that is, the king — claimed the right to *all* property as belonging to the kingdom. Therefore, in that time and culture, kings had a just claim on any produce that came from the fields. In short, the land was the king's, so the fruit from the land was entirely his, and anything the individual was allowed to keep was only by the king's grace.

When we worship with our tithing, we are giving a *spiritual* acknowledgment to this same concept, but at a larger, higher level. We are saying more — that *life* is a gift of God!

- Every time I tithe, I'm affirming again that everything I have comes from God.

- My first 10 percent is presented as an evidence of my recognition of that fact.

In the light of the human concept of "the king's portion," it's worthy to note how *little* our loving God actually mandates. He might have called for a larger, almost faith-exhausting starting place, but He only calls for the *tithe* — 10 percent. Plus, in the *human* tradition, kings generally gave nothing in return for receiving their portion. However, in the divine tradition, our beneficient and loving Father-Creator *insists* on responding to our giving. Even when we give a tithe, which is rightfully His, He opens the windows of heaven and abounds toward us. So think of it, loved one. If our tithes bring such a joyous response from the Father, imagine how He feels about offerings — and what He'll do when we are released to learn new levels of giving!

A Sweet Aroma

Offerings tend to be a rather "unknown quantity" in giving. Since a definite amount is not defined in Scripture, the amount we give in offerings can be treated too casually if we allow ourselves to be unthinking. Some may view offerings only as something to do with extra change in their pockets.

Others may round up their tithe checks to the nearest zero and say, "That's my offering." But because the Lord places such importance on the practice and spirit of giving offerings, we are wise to think more carefully about them.

How might we gain a grasp of the significance of presenting our offerings to the Lord?

Numbers 28:1-2 may provide a helpful guideline.

> Now the Lord spoke to Moses, saying, "Command the children of Israel, and say to them, 'My offering, My food for My offerings made by fire as a sweet aroma to Me, you shall be careful to offer to Me at their appointed time.' "

The Lord's command to Israel regarding their offerings especially noted that they were "a sweet aroma" to Him; that is, they simply gave Him pleasure. So God directed that, if the people did give, they were to "be careful" in such giving. And they were to bring them at their "appointed times."

On the face of it, God might sound demanding, as though to say, "I want *offerings* — and I want them *now!*" But a thoughtful analysis of the text brings clarity and helps us understand two or three things about presenting our offerings to the Lord. And as we do, we can be joyous in worship, knowing they will produce "a sweet aroma" to Him. Let me introduce a New Testament text and give an illustration.

First, the idea of an offering being a sweet aroma is as consistent with New Testament teaching as with the Old. In his letter to the Philippians, Paul expressly acknowledges their loving offerings to support his missionary ministry as "a sweet-smelling aroma, an acceptable sacrifice, well pleasing to God" (Phil. 4:18).

The congregation in Philippi was a gentile church, so we can be certain that the apostle wasn't using this term simply because it was a part of an understood Jewish tradition.

Instead, this terminology directly brings the Old Testament concept of offerings as "a sweet aroma unto God" into the realm of New Testament living and giving.

A Fair Question

But, someone may ask, if this relates to unrequired, free-will giving, how is it that God says to be careful and to make offerings at appointed times?

It's a fair question. And there is a good answer — one that keeps the focus on the "freewill" nature of our giving while still showing the wisdom in the Father's words to us.

First, God isn't issuing a demand. Rather, He's giving instruction to help us when we *do* decide to give. Why? Because even when a voluntary action is taken, it needs to be taken with the reverence and soberness appropriate to the One to whom we are presenting our offerings. And if God doesn't teach us how to give, who will?

An appropriate picture of this need for care is in the process of international protocol which is usually observed by mutual agreement between nations. When dignitaries — especially heads of state — visit from other lands, an entire body of procedures is carefully observed. This is *not* because they are *demanded* but because uncommon courtesy is appropriate by reason of the dignity of the office being acknowledged. If the president of the United States visits Brazil, or vice versa, the respective state departments see that the reception of the leader upon arrival and during the visit is afforded proper respect, timing and attentiveness.

Now, *we* are talking about bringing our offerings to the God of the universe! How appropriate it is that our mood and manner be gauged accordingly! Very!

I remember a man who visited the very first service Anna and I conducted in that little church in Indiana years ago. He was a funny old geezer, and that made his peculiar actions understandable. But that day, when the offering plate came by him, he literally "flipped" in a dime! He wasn't a poor man, so the amount was certainly inappropriate. And he was in a worship service, so the way he presented his offering was unworthy as well.

It's a rather humorous memory, but it's also a sad illustration. It is a reminder that my actions may not be the same as his, but when an opportunity for "presenting an offering" occurs, my mood and manner could be less than "a sweet aroma" to God. That's why I think the Lord says, "Be careful." He isn't mandating an offering. He's cautioning against reckless attitudes when we do give because our fallen nature may at times be less than appropriately sensitive to the dignity of the One to whom we give.

The Lord's words about our offerings being at an "appointed time" are worth considering, too. Let me illustrate.

There are certain times of the year when Anna doesn't *demand* a gift from me, but she is surely *delighted* when I give her one. And in most cases, timing is what makes the gift so delightful. On Valentine's Day, our anniversary or her birthday, the "appointed time" is significant, and the relevance of the gift is somehow diminished if I miss the timing.

Similarly, there are *times* when our offerings are a special delight. The timeliness of the Philippians' gift to Paul was acknowledged. In the same way, there are special times 1) in our churches, 2) in the face of need or tragedy or 3) in the Holy Spirit dealing with us and calling us to faith — times of God's appointment.

Thus, God's Word makes clear that the giving of offerings, though distinct and separate from the giving of tithes, is a vital part of our worship, and that in giving our offerings we are acknowledging the worthiness of the Lord. "Give to the Lord the glory due His name; bring an offering, and come into His courts" (Ps. 96:8).

True "Freewill" Offerings

In the Old Testament, the giving of offerings was an integral part of the sacrificial system. Burnt offerings and sin offerings were made for the forgiveness and the covering of sins. But other offerings served an entirely different purpose. Freewill offerings were given out of the overflow of a heart filled with gratefulness for all the Lord had done. Some offerings sealed a vow (Lev. 7:16). Others were made at times of high celebration (Lev. 23); still others out of thankfulness (Lev. 22:29).

The book of Malachi, which has traditionally been thought of as dealing only with tithing, also has much to say on the subject of the giving of offerings.

"Who is there even among you who would shut
   the doors,
So that you would not kindle fire on My altar in
   vain?
I have no pleasure in you,"
Says the Lord of hosts.
"Nor will I accept an offering from your hands.
For from the rising of the sun, even to its going
   down,
My name shall be great among the Gentiles;
In every place, incense shall be offered to My
   name,
And a pure offering;
For My name shall be great among the nations,"
   says the Lord of hosts.

"But you profane it,
In that you say,
'The table of the Lord is defiled;
And its fruit, its food, is contemptible.'
You also say,

'Oh, what a weariness!'
And you sneer at it,"
Says the Lord of hosts.
"And you bring the stolen, the lame, and the sick;
Thus you bring an offering!
Should I accept this from your hand?"
Says the Lord (Mal. 1:10-13).

In this text the Lord is dealing sternly with the sin of a people. Their selfishness became scorn. They brought the weak and lame of their flocks as "offerings" to the Lord — the animals they wanted to get rid of anyway. Therefore, they had no personal expense.

- They were offering to the Lord of heaven that which was worthless.

- They were going through the mere form of worship without the spirit of worship.

They were doing precisely what David refused to do, for he reverenced God too greatly.

Nor will I offer burnt offerings to the Lord my God
with that which costs me nothing (2 Sam. 24:24).

Free From Guilt-giving

Let's consider another area regarding our giving of offerings: the special *appeals* we often encounter.

We've all been faced with fundraising methodology that uses guilt as a means to get people to give. For example, this is often seen in efforts to raise money for orphanages in the Orient, earthquake victims in Guatemala or refugees of a typhoon in Bangladesh.

People tend to give more readily to such needs, and that's

wonderful. But in some cases, their motivation to give may not be soundly based. Why? Because sometimes we who live in relative affluence compared to most of the world can be "bought off" by a sense of guilt for our "having" in the midst of so many "have-nots" in the world.

Of course, compassion is appropriate.

And giving out of our abundance is proper.

But such offerings ought to be administrated in a spirit of gratitude, not guilt. God does not call us — *ever* — to live under any kind of condemnation. Learning to live in abundance is right, because to learn abundance is to learn to minister out of that resource with a sense of privilege, not shame. The God of plenty — our loving Father — wants to teach us the privilege of *responsible distribution*. It's the *joy* of people like us, who have so much even when we have little, to give from the abundant resources God has released to us.

The attitude behind the giving of our offerings is the most important aspect of this part of our worship. It is clear from Jesus' own teachings that the amount is not what brings God's favor, but what is in our hearts.

> For they all put in out of their abundance, but she out of her poverty put in all that she had, her whole livelihood (Mark 12:44).

> For the Lord does not see as man sees; for man looks at the outward appearance, but the Lord looks at the heart (1 Sam. 16:7).

God calls us to cheerful-heart giving (2 Cor. 9:7) and reminds us that the true sacrifices of God are "a broken spirit, a broken and a contrite heart" (Ps. 51:17).

In short, God never wants — nor will His Spirit ever motivate — giving through guilt or mere obligation. Instead, He wants to multiply our resources and then call us to new steps of faith and worship, in which offerings regularly flow from our hands. He wants to purify our hearts — to bring us to a place where we can offer to the Lord *often* "an offering in righteousness" (Mal. 3:3).

Three Categories

The Bible describes three different kinds of offerings: 1) offerings of the firstfruits of our labors, 2) offerings of humanitarian relief and 3) offerings given for the spread of the gospel.

Firstfruits

The Lord commanded Israel, "The first of the firstfruits of your land you shall bring into the house of the Lord your God" (Ex. 23:19). This directive was further elaborated on in Deuteronomy 18:4:

> The firstfruits of your grain and your new wine and your oil, and the first of the fleece of your sheep, you shall give him.

Living in a nonagricultural society as we do, it is sometimes unclear how these commands are to be implemented in our lives. But the message was clear to Israel: They were not only to tithe on all of their increase, but they were to give an additional offering on any increase that was over and above that of the year before.

This is something our family has practiced for years. Whenever a raise or a bonus has been received, we give an extra gift *beyond* our tithe. We don't have a set percentage that we use, but we ask the Lord to show us what we are to do in each situation.

Humanitarian Gifts

> He who has pity on the poor lends to the Lord, and
> He will pay back what he has given (Prov. 19:17).

This verse sets the tone for God's view of our responsibility toward all humankind. The Lord even goes so far as to say that how we give to the poor reflects our respect for Him.

> He who oppresses the poor reproaches his Maker,
> but he who honors Him has mercy on the needy
> (Prov. 14:31).

The apostle James later taught that our obligation goes beyond the spiritual and into the physical realm.

> If a brother or sister is naked and destitute of daily
> food, and one of you says to them, "Depart in
> peace, be warmed and filled," but you do not give
> them the things which are needed for the body,
> what does it profit? Thus also faith by itself, if it
> does not have works, is dead (James 2:15-17).

Thus we are commanded to care for those in need. But here again, God does not call for this without the promise of reward! As we've seen in Proverbs 19, giving to the poor is a "loan to the Lord," and make no mistake — God pays back with interest! That's why the Word of God adds that "he who gives to the poor will not lack" (Prov. 28:27). Note that such promises do not cheapen our giving, but they glorify the God of our salvation who is so generous, so loving and so practical!

One year I decided to tabulate for about three weeks every letter that came to my house asking for a charitable donation or a gift, either from a Christian group or from a charitable organization in our society. In less than a month, I received twenty-two letters of appeal for support.

I kept this data for a combination of reasons. First, I did it for my own information because I had long before made a decision that I would not label as "junk mail" any letter that came 1) asking for help in spreading the gospel or 2) asking for help for people who were in need or pain. I also recognized that since I wouldn't *call* it junk mail, I couldn't *treat* it like junk mail; therefore, I had to make a decision about each letter that arrived.

Let me describe what arrived in that three-week period. I received appeals from eight evangelistic ministries and five were from what I call "mercy ministries" — feeding ministries, prison ministries, downtown missions and so forth. Further, I received five others from organizations having to do with human affliction — for example, Disabled American Veterans, the Heart Association, the March of Dimes and so on. Finally, four were from specialized Christian ministries in literature or the media which were not evangelistic but were more specialized efforts in evangelism (for example, missionary radio outreaches).

How did I decide which to support?

First, I decided on the basis of *relationship.*

Of these twenty-two, there were only nine with whom I felt any personal sense of familiarity or personal "call" to partnership. Although I had heard of the programs or the leaders from all nine, only five were ones I felt akin to. I'd given to them before. The other four simply arrived in the mail. They weren't unworthy, but I would not be ruled by guilt or obligation in making the decision to give or not. Since I didn't perceive any sense of personal mission which called for my prayerful consideration, I gave first where *relationship* — a sense of God-given "partnership" — recommended it.

Second, I gave where *responsibility* seemed appropriate.

For example, I always try to send some amount to groups

which help people who hurt, even if that amount is only a couple of dollars to cover their mailing costs. But I'll give more in other cases.

Take the Disabled American Veterans, for example. I find myself incapable of not responding to their appeals. They are asking for help to defray some of the extra costs of caring for people who have lost limbs or been disabled in some way because they defended my country. Because I enjoy freedom at the expense of these who paid in life and limb, I feel a sense of responsibility to give.

Third, I gave where *gratitude* recommends it.

I always give to the March of Dimes. If it weren't for the healing power of God, I would have been crippled or dead from infantile paralysis (polio). The March of Dimes was originally founded to raise money for polio research, but now, since polio has been conquered, they concentrate on birth defects. So, out of thankfulness to God, I give to this organization. Though it is not a "spiritual" enterprise in the sense of being a church-oriented ministry, my gratitude to God summons my giving.

Helping the Spread of the Gospel

Giving to God's work and His workers is nothing new in Scripture. In Moses' time the priests were not only provided for by the congregation, but

> Everyone came whose heart was stirred, and every-one whose spirit was willing, and they brought the Lord's offering for the work of the tabernacle of meeting, for all its service, and for the holy garments (Ex. 35:21).

Later, the New Testament talks not only about the church giving to the needy (2 Cor. 8:1-7), but also providing people and funds for the spreading of the gospel (Acts 15:22). So the precedent was set. And the pattern has been established in

God's Word regarding how churches and gospel ministries are to function financially.

I remember hearing Charles Fuller, usually called the founder of worldwide media evangelism, speaking on tithes and offerings. Even though he ran the risk of ransacking his support base, he taught that the tithes of God's people were to be placed into "the storehouse" — that is, given to the church where each believer received his or her nourishment and fellowship in Christ. Then, with heart-touching passion, this great man called for people of faith to rise up with offerings of love to spread the gospel by all means possible — missions, media and ministry of every manner. As a pastor, I've always appreciated this instruction I received as a child from a man who was the "Billy Graham" of a preceeding generation.

As a Pastor...

I consistently deal with the temptation to worry about teaching what I've just written. Just as we may be tempted to hesitate in giving because we're afraid we won't have enough left, as a pastor, I've had to resist the same temptation regarding the giving our church does. Every pastor has to face the temptation to protect his congregation against outside appeals, as though their larger trans-church giving would drain the local coffers.

But I think I've *won*. I think the temptation to become self-centered, focusing on our own local ministry, has been smashed. And I'm happy that our congregation gives away a very large percentage of our local church budget every week, month and year.

There is too much of a tendency to have a poverty mentality in today's church. You and I are both tempted by it, regardless of our profession. Our outlook is too small, but that smallness can be shaken off in answer to our Lord Jesus, who has called us to be *big* people.

153

Big in our world view.

Big in our love for the lost.

Big in our giving.

A large banner hangs in the front of our youth group meeting room. On it are emblazoned just two words: *Be Huge!*

That's what our Savior has called us to be — big enough to embrace a world with arms that are open in love and with hands that have learned to give.

They're hands that have learned to hold without "clutching." I began understanding that fact through an experience I had while in college.

TWELVE

POSSESSING
OR POSSESSED

*God never tells us
that we can't have
dreams, desires,
longings or fulfillment.
He only warns us against
being controlled by
the fear of not having
them on our schedule
or of seeking them
on our own terms.*

WHILE I was in college, I was a regular part of a Christian broadcast production team on a Los Angeles radio station. Our organist was a talented man of many gifts, making a donation of his time to the broadcast. One day, as he was playing a song that was familiar to me, he did something unfamiliar — he employed an absolutely magnificent chord progression that I'd never heard before. It was stunning — I almost felt as though I'd discovered "the lost chord"!

After the broadcast, I went over to the organist and asked, "Ed, you know that progression you did on 'Now I Belong to Jesus'? It was gorgeous! Would you show me how to play it?"

He looked up from the keyboard and, with no change of expression, simply said, "No."

I honestly thought he was joking, so I laughed and said, "Come on, Ed, show me."

But to my utter amazement, the man looked back at me, leveled his gaze and, not with cruelty but with a very starchy tone and matching facial expression, repeated, "No." Then he added, "I don't show people those things."

It was an awkward, completely surprising moment. I didn't feel angry with him, but I was amazed — feeling poorer for having asked.

About three years later I was in a church where I heard that same progression played by a pianist, but on another song. After the service I went to the person who had been at the piano, introduced myself and asked, "Would you play the chord sequence you used on..." and I named the song. "Could you show me how to do that?"

"Sure," he said. "C'mon and sit down, and I'll do that."

He was cheerful and assisting, and when I sat down on the bench beside him, he carefully "walked me through" the progression. Then he showed me its use in other songs — how to apply the nuance *any* place I wanted.

As years have gone by, I've often looked back on those two occasions and truly felt sorry for the first man. And I've wondered how much of life Ed might have missed for being so protective of his gifts. I've also wondered to myself how much "music," that is, "creativity," is in every one of us. How much *ministry*, how many *resources, talents* and *abilities* do we have that our human fears or stubbornness force us to hold in reserve? How often might there come an opportunity for you or me to give away, to share; yet for whatever reason, we clutch what we have to ourselves?

There's a name for that "clutchiness."

It isn't nice.

Covetousness.

Covetousness hides and survives in all of us to some degree. We may tend to think of it as applying only to financial or material areas, but covetousness and possessiveness have to do with any gift we hold back on — "getting and keeping" or, like Ed, "having it, but only for myself." This spirit can infect any area of our lives when we yield to subtle or not-so-subtle feelings of the need to secure ourselves.

Recognizing Covetousness

With a student, it might manifest itself in the hoarding of source material for a term paper, telling no one else about a great research source he's discovered. Why? He might try to find a rationale for "keeping it all." For example, "I wouldn't want the teacher to think that we'd copied each other's papers." The mind conjures up a self-justifying excuse, but the real reason is *competition*; the quest for an opportunity to stand in advantage above others by means of something we have that others don't; something that distinguishes us by either diminishing others or leaving them in our dust. This type of spirit makes us clinch our fists even tighter to hold on to whatever it is we have.

An artist may come up with a combination of oils to create a distinct hue. But when asked how she developed that shade, she replies, "Ah, that's my secret!" What apparently doesn't occur to her is that the living God who gifted her — the God who paints the sky in ten thousand locations every day, with ten thousand different mixtures of color and uniqueness — that God could creatively *give her even more* new mixtures in oils. The price of that possibility, however, is her remembering that 1) He is the *Source* of her imagination, 2) the gifts are from Him for *her* to freely give, and 3) she will discover unending gifts from Him if she releases the flow by giving away what He gave her. But when the artist, the student, the organist — *anyone of us!* — allow room for possessiveness — that is, covetousness — it limits our creative potential.

How about recipes?

"Oh, I could never share that. It's a family secret!"

And like the artist, another person loses the access to marvelous and infinite creative possibilities that arise from God begetting more and more in them, more than ever existed in their families, more than ever imagined in their lives! The fear of losing "what I have" blocks the door to "what I can become." Yet all the while, the Creator of *everything* offers the Key to it all: Turn *everything* about your life over to Me; learn to give as you've been given to, and discover the unlimited possibilities I can beget in and through you.

He is a God of *resource-fullness*.

With Him as our Source, we can never lack for anything needed — or *new* — because He's the One able to make something out of nothing every day! Hear it! And *know* the Creator is not a past-tense Creator. He's our Father *today*, "who gives life to the dead and calls those things which do not exist as though they did" (Rom. 4:17). This truth calls us to the place of decision: Will I live my life in relationship to My Creator's endless resources, or will I keep restricting myself to the limits of my own resources?

These observations bring us face-to-face with our *attitudes*. But they also call for *answers* about our finances and possessions. Or, more accurately, answers to help us find out whether we're being practical or possessive about certain matters.

Nothing more touches the nerve of impending covetousness than the fear we've all felt: Will I have enough? It starts in our childhood with a slowness to share toys or candy. We then "grow" and learn the uneasiness about sharing a friend — the feelings of jealousy, coveting *all* attention and interest for ourselves. We withhold acceptance, hold back on generosity, refuse a compliment, grouse at offering time. And finally, before we realize it, this oh-so-human pattern has come to dominate our lives.

It climaxes in our drawing back from surrendering to God's will: If I do *that* I won't get to do or have what *I* want. I may try and convince myself I'm only hesitating in "giving Him my all" until I'm sure that *first* there's some guarantee assuring my security, certainty of contentment and so forth. But I'm only blocking the way to blessing, because life in His kingdom never works that way. He calls us *out* to give ourselves *over* to His will and with no guarantees — only His promises. And even then He doesn't promise a gold mine in any or in every mountain that He calls us to climb with Him. But He *does* promise that if a mountain gets in the way of His purposed fulfillment for our lives, He can move it!

God never disallows dreams. In fact, He gives them. So He'll never tell us that we can't have dreams, desires, longings or fulfillment. He only warns us against being controlled by the fear of not having them on our schedule or of seeking them on our own terms.

Jesus said, "One's life does not consist in the abundance of the things he possesses" (Luke 12:15). And if we *ever* put our resources, trust, confidence, identities or security in anything other than Him, to that exact degree those things will become a substitute for Him. He won't allow that. It's the reason a covetous man is called an "idolater" (Eph. 5:5). The desperation and nervousness — the *need* to "have" that taunts us all — gradually will crowd Him out completely. That's why possessiveness in any disguise must be identified, confronted and surrendered. It's essential to our gaining the Key to Everything.

Self-examining Inquiry

The human capacity for being so easily caught in the trap of our own possessiveness, and the quest to turn from that, calls us to an entire arena of self-examining inquiry.

- How much of my own money is it right for me to enjoy?

- How much is acceptable to have in the bank without being guilty of "laying up for yourself" in the way Jesus discouraged?

- How much should I set aside to plan for retirement?

- Is it unbelieving of me to have insurance?

- What if I have several more suits or dresses than some other people do?

- Is it OK to invest in the stock market?

- What about owning a house instead of renting, or the other way around?

- Will I displease God if I have *anything?*

The list could go on almost indefinitely because daily occurrences bring to light unending possibilities for giving or keeping.

Are there any conclusive answers to these questions?

No. No, because ultimately every one of these issues is a *heart* matter. They can't be ruled on externally by human programs of legal allowance or disallowance. They're only answered from within as I honest-to-God address myself with the question: Am I motivated by fear — the need to *have* — or am I motivated by a sound-minded, faith-in-God-based, practical wisdom?

Making decisions on such things as those listed above is *not* really a question of is it sin or not — at least not in the sense of sin being evil or even selfish. But these questions call us to let the Holy Spirit keep a monitor on our motives. He's the One who knows what motivates us — even better than *we* do! And He'll help us if we'll let Him; He'll help our thinking, planning, purchasing and provisioning for our present or future.

I think the Word of God is clear on this: He would not want people to carry any sense of guilt or condemnation because they have savings, investments, retirement plans or insurance. These resources are not a measure of whether or not a person trusts the Lord. They are matters on which you and I each individually need to satisfy our own conscience before Him, for as Romans 14:22 says, "Happy is he who does not condemn himself in what he approves."

The Bible gives numerous examples and directives about such matters, but they focus on practical balance, not prohibitions. For example:

- Jesus describes as a "fool" a man who made great plans for preserving his future against poverty but who left God out of His agenda and ended up with no future at all (Luke 12:16-21).

- Yet in the same Gospel, our Lord commends careful planning and taking stock of future needs in order to avoid embarrassment or loss (Luke 14:25-33).

The latter text referenced, in which Jesus commends "counting the cost," is His call to look fully and only to the Lord in your life commitments and decisions. "Whoever of you does not forsake all that He has cannot be My disciple" (Luke 14:33).

Surrender.

It's the same issue we'll always face once we open up to Jesus and His ways; when the Key to Everything seeks to unlock us from anything that would haunt or torment us with empty suppositions. The issue isn't *what you have* but *what has you?* Better yet, *who?*

Once the issue of *ownership* is settled, life's what-can-I-have questions are settled with it.

- I have been bought with a price; I am not my own (1 Cor. 6:20).

- All that I have I've been given; I am only a steward of that trust (1 Chron. 29:14).

- Therefore, I can have "all things to enjoy" because nothing rules me, and I am an avenue for God to minister things to others through me (1 Tim. 6:17; Eph. 4:28).

Thus we'll find that as we view our "havings" or "holdings" in God's kingdom ways, we can plan for our future in freedom and faith. Then, no matter what we do, we'll always recognize *Him* as being our ultimate Provider, no matter what we have. We'll have understood that we will *never* be able to *save* enough, *invest* enough, *plan* enough or in *any* way build up enough support of human adequacy. We'll have learned that His promises and presence are our only sure support for the future.

Banks fail. Investments fall apart. The continuous climb of inflation reduces the power of money saved today against tomorrow. These facts *don't* argue against saving or investment, but they *do* remind us it's impossible to ever be truly secure on earth's terms.

But once our trust is fixed completely in God, our living, loving Father will show us the way to exercise our personal responsibilities. He'll teach us how to be wise, disciplined and faithful as His stewards, looking toward our future with faith, not fear.

Joseph is a prime example of someone who prepared for the future (see Gen. 41-42). Yet, please note that Joseph prepared, not out of fear, but out of divine direction. God told him what to do, and he did precisely that.

Jeremiah, too, provided for his future by protecting legal papers that would identify him as the rightful owner to certain properties (Jer. 32:1-15). He knew that Israel would go into captivity, but he also knew by "the word of the Lord" that they would return. So as an act of faith, Jeremiah purchased a property and got his papers in legal order, knowing that the day would come when the land would be possessed again. The prophet's actions are a practical application of Proverbs 13:22, which says that we should consider laying up an inheritance for our children.

On the other hand, Jesus said, "Do not worry about tomorrow" (Matt. 6:34). But He wasn't saying we shouldn't plan or make any calculations about the future. He was saying not to let our minds be hassled or pressed by how we're going to make it. In other words, we aren't to plan for our future in fear, doubt or with selfish concern. But we're to seek the Lord for specific direction and guidance, realizing that He will preserve both — our future and our present (Matt. 6:33). Then we're ready to carry out His purposes in confidence and faith.

Functioning in Faith

Functioning in faith when it comes to our finances can be a very sensitive subject. I've often been troubled over a superficial mentality that seems to have been bred into some people's minds by what is called "prosperity teaching."

First, let me say (of course!) God *does* want us to prosper!

It would be less than biblical to deny that God makes very practical covenants with His people — promises that if we will learn the grace of generosity and obedience in giving, He'll abound toward us.

And He *keeps* those promises, too.

However, sweeping generalizations about God's "promises of abundance" easily distort the full scope of the Bible's teaching. Too often they completely overlook the New Testament's call to a spirit of sacrifice, to self-giving service or to communal suffering. Some deny these ideas too readily, almost mocking them by their cavalier abandon. And when this happens, God's true promises of plenty, along with His stated will to bless and prosper His people, end up reduced to self-centered slogans and spiritualized get-rich-quick schemes.

God *never* said His people would not have money.

He *never* said His people would not own property.

He *never* said His people couldn't have fine cars and clothes.

But by the same token, neither did He say that the verification of their faith would ever be having life's material comforts. He hasn't ordained us to prosperity with an eye to us spending our lives wallowing in the gravy of abundance. Instead, He wants us to learn His ways of prosperity so that His abundance can be entrusted to us. He does this so that we can distribute it *all the more abundantly*; to be His hand of distribution to as many as possible who need, whether that need is for His life, His love or His provision in their material circumstances.

Experiencing *His* Joy

Several years ago I received a check from somebody who wrote, "Jack, the Lord told me to send you this." It was a cashier's check for $155. It seemed an odd amount to me, and, moreover, I felt embarrassed because I didn't need it. I've often had something given to me which precisely matched a need, but this time I didn't have a $155-need that I could identify.

I thought, "Maybe something is coming up — trouble with the car or something like that — and the Lord is providing the funds ahead of time." So I laid the check on the dresser at home and waited.

About two days later I got a letter from a friend who was in a real financial pinch. "Lord," I prayed, "is this why You gave me this money ahead of time?"

The strongest impression occurred within my mind: *Yes, so you could have the joy of distributing it!*

It was a simple but memorable lesson to me. I was helped to recognize how much God delights to give to us at times, not for ourselves, but to partner with Him; to allow us the pleasure of experiencing something of *His* great joy in providing for others!

I think He wants to teach all of us that joy because He has an incredible bounty to give! And He's looking for people through whom He can flow that bounty.

The Bible says He's called us to be "kings" (Rev. 1:6), and there's more to being a king than merely sitting selfishly in the middle of your own abundance. Faithful kings are concerned for people. And as "kings" under the headship of the King of kings, we must learn how to function with and manage abundance in the interest of others.

The Early Church and Possessions

Let me deal with one last point regarding the what-can-I-have question

Scriptural accounts of the early church have always held great fascination for any who want to experience the New Testament lifestyle to its fullest. Worship, miracles and take-God-at-His-Word boldness are exciting aspects of dynamic Christianity we'd all like to see developed in our own lives. But in Acts 4 we encounter a situation that appears almost *un*natural, rather than supernatural.

The Bible reports that these early believers were readily selling their things so they could share together.

Now the multitude of those who believed were of one heart and one soul; neither did anyone say that

> any of the things he possessed was his own, but
> they had all things in common. And with great
> power the apostles gave witness to the resurrection
> of the Lord Jesus. And great grace was upon them
> all. Nor was there anyone among them who lacked;
> for all who were possessors of land or houses sold
> them, and brought the proceeds of the things that
> were sold, and laid them at the apostles' feet; and
> they distributed to each as anyone had need (Acts
> 4:32-35).

What are the implications of this text for committed believers today? What was the Spirit doing *then*, and what does that mean for us *now?*

Perhaps an important beginning point of understanding is noticing that their actions were *voluntary*, not required or regimented.

> Neither did anyone say that any of the things he
> possessed was his own, but they had all things in
> common (v. 32).

Does that mean that everyone concluded, "I can't have anything because I have to give it all to God?" No, not at all.

Instead, this action in the early church was surprisingly simple. Apparently, as the Lord prompted different people, they individually, on their own advisement, would take some of their possessions and sell them. Then they would bring these resources and place them in a common "pool" under the discretionary care of the apostles to be distributed as need arose. What they did is not recorded as being *commanded*, but as a spontaneous action of their own.

Further, the broader picture in the New Testament doesn't suggest that this is something everyone did. Nor even that everyone who *did* so, sold *everything* he had. (You'll note that Ananias and Sapphira were not judged for not giving everything. That wasn't required — see Acts 5:4a. But what they *were* judged for was *claiming* to give all, when, in fact, they had withheld a portion. Their judgment was for *lying*, not for *having*.)

The primary message inherent in this whole picture is the testimony of God's love at work, of people who have a *practical* as well as a *spiritual* concern for each other. But their material sharing was entirely spiritual at its root and not legislated by the apostles. It was a voluntary expression from people 1) who knew their Source, 2) who were filled with the Spirit's love and 3) who wanted to see each other cared for so unselfishly that, like Jesus, they were willing to lay down anything in order to see it happen.

Are we obligated to this same action today? Should we expect this kind of thing from people who seek to live "in the Spirit"?

Let's start our answer by affirming that this New Testament practice should *not* be argued away. It's valid. And we *ought* to let the Lord orchestrate such care for each other among us today as well.

But at the same time, this text shouldn't be extrapolated to suggest a humanistic, communistic system aimed at making everyone fiscal equals. Their sharing together was not designed to bring everyone to the lowest common denominator. It wasn't a silly we'll-all-have-the-same-thing, all-wear-the-same-color-clothes, and all-buy-our-things-at-the-same-co-op socialistic monstrosity. Instead, their practice teaches us more of a mind-set than a method.

When the love of God wells up in the hearts of a group of His children, they will more than likely show a willingness to freely share what they have. It's the lifestyle of love. We *received* when we *believed*, so now we *give* as a way to *live*. That's what they did at the church's beginning. And that's all that any of us are asked to do today.

No heavenly law dictates that we sell everything we have,

cloister ourselves in a commune and live on organically grown vegetables and goat's milk. That's been done in forced ways, and it doesn't work. Forced ways never work because that's not how God does things. Rather, He calls us to be salt and light *everywhere*, and much of what "shines" through us of His light will be in the way we handle *everything*. His spirit of loving, giving and sharing among and through His people is one of His primary means for "lighting the world" (Matt. 5:16).

The Rich Young Ruler

Have you ever become nervous while reading the story of the young ruler? (Matt. 19:16-22) Jesus told him, "Sell what you have and give to the poor...and come, follow Me" (v. 21). Was this a norm Jesus meant to establish? Is this Christ's call to everyone today?

Again, the answers are in looking at the *heart* issue rather than in establishing this case as a precedent for every single one of Jesus' followers.

Jesus was reading the man's heart. His words were meant to cut to the core of a problem in that particular man's life. The Bible says, "He went away sorrowful for he had great possessions" (v. 22).

Do you see the *real* problem? The man's money wasn't his problem; his mind-set was. He was no longer free. His possessions *possessed him*, rather than him possessing his possessions.

Jesus goes on to say that we can easily become dominated by the things we have. He didn't ask the young man to give all as though it's a timeless law for verifying a person's sincerity in wanting to follow Him: Get rid of everything and prove you love Me! No.

And yet, while a "test" of our spirituality is not "passed" by selling things that we have, such a test can become a point of confronting in us what the young ruler discovered: He was

cwned by "things." And what frees us from having to have —
and frees us to *have* so we can *give* — is our being *un-*
owned by anything or anyone but Christ.

That was the foundation for the early church's understanding. There we see a people living in the spirit of free-
handed distribution, as a giving, ministering people. The
foundation for that atmosphere was their Holy-Spirit-begot-
ten recognition of God alone as their Source and their willingness to be a channel for His use. This is the basic point of
understanding if we're interested in learning the financial life
of the early church.

The bottom-line issue is this: If I've been *born* into the life
of the kingdom, do I *function* in the spirit of the kingdom?
That's the summons to each of us — and once we start, the
Holy Spirit won't let us go back easily.

I know you can't *really* go back.

I tried.

It was a long time ago.

Mad at God

It was a tough time for our young family. We'd just had our
third baby in less than five years, and the budget was
stretched way beyond its limits. The only way we survived
was through the blessing of honorariums — the unrequired
but graciously given checks I received for speaking engage-
ments I had. I was serving at the Foursquare Church head-
quarters at the time as the national youth director for our
denomination. The position was impressive in title, but the
salary was modest, to say the least.

Anna and I lived gratefully and completely without ex-
travagance, and we had to be practical in all our spending.
Anna has always been creative in making our house's appearance and our family's nutrition program both pleasant
and satisfying on limited funds. At Christmas she would even
make most of the gifts we gave by the skill of her own

handiwork. So our financial pinch at this particular time wasn't due to carelessness.

I just had not had a speaking engagement for two months. And nothing was on the calendar for the next two months, either. But that was only half the situation. There was another side to the problem.

Even though our funds were low, we had continued to give our tithe. And we had also continued to give our extra 5 percent to missions during this "pinch" — that is, until something happened.

It was early September. After I'd deposited my paycheck at the first of the month, I had written our usual check to the church for our tithe. (I would never even think of not doing that!)

But I had entertained other thoughts.

I had decided, "Our funds are so low that I'm not going to give to the missionary program this month. After all, that's not a requirement, and we're in a tight spot." So I hadn't added the extra 5 percent for our missionary "faith promise."

But the extra money didn't seem to help much. (It's amazing how small the resource pool is when you try to fill it yourself!) It was the day after Labor Day, and, with a three-week-old baby in the house, new expenses were piling up.

Suddenly I exploded.

I've never before nor since demonstrated such direct anger at God. I surprised myself. I embarrassed myself, too, as suddenly, alone in the living room with my mind pressed and stressed over bills, I *shouted* at the top of my voice: *"GOD, IT'S NOT FAIR!"*

I had all kinds of thoughts in my mind, but primarily I was mad. My emotions were pitched to a fever level as I reasoned my complaint: We *have* been faithful to *tithe*, and now *God* isn't coming through with the *goods!*

But almost as quickly as I had shouted, that still, small voice whispered back in response to my charge of His not being fair: "Neither is it fair that you have withheld your offerings to Me."

If someone had dropped a boulder on my head, it couldn't have stopped me any quicker in my tracks, nor shaken me any harder. My reaction was instant.

I started to cry.

I cried hard.

I wandered into the kitchen and leaned on the stove, telling God how sorry I was for my outburst, and how stupid I felt for having doubted Him. I recited some of the many times He had seen us through —

> fantastically,
>> miraculously,
>>> faithfully,
>>>> lovingly —

and I told Him I was *glad* for the words He spoke back to me.

I was glad He wouldn't let me "go back." It was a moving thing to know my Father would not allow me to shrink back to a former size in my faith or my life of stewardship. I was happy He "cared enough to send the very best" in sending Jesus; happy He wouldn't let me give less than my best in following Him.

The story ends predictably.

That same day I wrote a check for our missionary giving, and the next day the phone on my desk began to jingle with invitations to come and minister. Of course, the greatest joy was the privilege of bringing the Word of God wherever I spoke, but the divine providence of God supplying for our growing family through the honorariums was not insignificant.

But beyond that immediate blessing was a lifelong lesson: *Giving* with Christ is like *living* with Him. Once you set out on the journey, there's no *real* way of turning back, not if you're going to follow the King.

Now let me ask you: Are you ready?

Are you ready to let the *life* in giving expand in you for a lifetime of joyous discoveries?

I hope so, because that's exactly what you'll find.

The Key to Everything that life has to offer is found in opening up to the full dimensions of God's love manifest in His Holy Spirit of giving.

You can carry that Key for all your *life* and exercise that Key for all its *power*. As long as you hold that Key with all your *heart*.

It's a heart-shaped key, you know; and the heart that learns to hold it has found the beginning *and* the ending of everything.

I'll tell you what I mean.

THIRTEEN

WHERE
EVERYTHING
ENDS...AND
BEGINS

*When you give
everything, it doesn't
make any difference
how much it is.
It's everything!*

I'LL NEVER know the exact amount. But I learned that it didn't really make any difference, and God told me why. It started with a one-hundred-dollar bill.

I can't remember where Anna and I got it. I think it was a gift in a Christmas card, but it's been several years now, and I don't recall. What I do remember is exchanging it for smaller currency.

We were just getting ready to leave for a three-day gathering of fellow pastors in Santa Barbara, California, and this was to be our spending money. I knew it wouldn't be very practical to walk into a restaurant and pull out a bill that size to pay a six- or seven-dollar breakfast check, so that's why I stopped at the bank to have it changed into smaller bills.

Because we had to stop and gas the car en route, the hundred dollars had been reduced. However, I had a few extra dollars in my wallet before I added the hundred. So after gassing up the car, I suppose I had something in the neighborhood of ninety to ninety-five dollars. Cash. Just for expenses. Some for fun.

That night the conference opened, and well into the worship service an offering was received. At first I hesitated to give at all because the conference was supposed to be funded by the registration fees of participants, and I'd paid Anna's and mine in advance.

But I changed my mind for two reasons.

First, I decided long ago that *anytime* I'm in a service and an offering is received, if I have *anything* at all, I'll give *some*thing. I *never* want to be a non-participant when an opportunity to give is provided.

Second, we had been worshipping. Beautifully. And I simply couldn't allow myself to separate the warmth of praise from the responsible privilege of giving. So I opened my wallet to take out a couple dollar bills. "Nope," I thought. "I need to do more than that."

Then I started to pull out a five-dollar bill, and I felt the same thing. And with that I was stopped. Somehow I was being prompted to *ask* what I should give.

To relate the story completely necessitates confessing the fact that I not only didn't *want* to ask, but I was puzzled by the whole process that was unfolding in my soul. After all, I thought, the conference is already paid for. Why the offering anyway? And why this strange prompting?

But deep inside I already knew the answer. Because the issue in *any* offering is the worship of the heart, not the expense that needs to be paid or the need that must be met. I knew that.

I also knew I was being called to *pray* — to specifically ask, "Lord, what do You want me to give in this offering?" When I did, the inner voice gave an instant answer: "Give it all."

Before I tell what happened next, and how I obeyed without hesitation, let me insert: Do you ever hesitate to ask God what you should give for fear He'll say exactly what He said to me then? I understand that.

And while I must say honestly that at my present stage of life I think I'm free from that fear, I can fully sympathize with anyone feeling it. That fear is prompted by two things: 1) the fear God will exploit us and 2) the fear we might "talk ourselves into something" which *God* didn't say but which our subconscious dictates.

Let me say it plainly, loved one: God will *never* capitalize on your vulnerability to His authority in your life. And further, even if your subconscious ever *did* "think up" an overly generous action on its own, be assured that God would *not* be so loveless as to leave it unrewarded.

Anyway, I was ready to obey — and the offering plate was getting close to me by now.

Quickly, I started to inconspicuously count how much was in my wallet. Don't ask me the reason. I just felt I'd like to know what I gave. But as I started to count, to get a quick mental calculation of the total I was preparing to put in the offering, the voice spoke again: "Just put it all in. When you give *everything*, it doesn't make any difference what the total is. It's *everything*."

I drew the small clump of bills from my wallet and put them in the plate. (The receptacle was actually a small bag, so I was able to place it all inside without anyone nearby seeing that small, but heftier-than-average wad of cash.) And as I sat there in the aftermath of that moment, I was struck by the profound simplicity of what the Holy Spirit had just taught me.

When you give everything, it doesn't make any difference how much it is. It's everything!

That simple statement is what this book has been about.

I've sought to share with you the lessons I've learned over a number of years of growth in understanding God's heart — about *everything*. I've tried to demonstrate from His Word that the Key to Everything centers on *giving*:

- on *for*giving because we've been forgiven,

- on *letting go* because we've been set free,

- on *giving up* because nothing's ever gained by holding back,

- and on *giving freely* because God has charged us nothing for all He's done for us or given to us.

I've sought to show the immediate relationship between finding the fullest release of God's purposes for our lives and learning the fullness of the *spirit* of release as we grow in giving.

And I'm about to conclude.

But before I do I want you to come with me to the most obvious place in the world for us to finish. It's the place where everything was *given*, everything was *finished* and everything can be *started*. All new.

Come there with me. To Calvary.

You know the words of that precious verse as well as I do. Let's say them together.

> For God so loved the world that He gave His only begotten Son, that whoever believes in Him should not perish but have everlasting life (John 3:16).

Let's say one more.

> He who did not spare His own Son, but delivered Him up for us all, how shall He not with Him freely give us all things (Rom. 8:32).

These are the greatest *giving* words in universal history because they declare the magnificence of what was *given*, *finished* and *started* at the cross of Jesus Christ.

- The life of God's Son was *given* so that a life for every one of us might be gained — *fully*.

- The plan, price and provision of salvation was *finished* so that God's plan for each of us could be afforded and received — *freely*.

- The hope of new birth and eternal life was *started* so that any one of us could enter God's kingdom now and, finally, enter heaven — *forever*.

It's the *shape* of the Key to Everything. The cross.

It's the fountainhead of all fullness in *everything* — from finding a fulfilled life, a fulfilling future and an eternity of fulfillment in the presence of the God who created us to know *Him*, His *richest* and His *best!*

And I want us to conclude there — worshipping. Because if you and I stay close to that cross and the Christ who died there and now lives forever, we'll never forget what was given at Calvary.

Everything.

And if we remember *that*,
- we'll always remember to *forgive*;
- we'll never be afraid to *give* and
- we'll have found the way to *live*.

We won't need to stop to count *anything* God asks us to do. It will never seem like a little or a lot to obey because our lives will be lived in the light of the cross — where *everything* takes on a different perspective.

And when we have learned to give as we have been given to, then our returning *everything* to Him won't ever require any tabulation or calculation because we'll be returning to Him in kind — *everything*.

Two Songs

The campfire was burning brightly in the center of that circle of teenage campers gathered in the high Sierra Mountains in central California. My fourteen-year-old voice was lifted right along with the rest of the kids:

> After all He's done for me,
> After all He's done for me,
>> How can I do less
>> Than give Him my best
>> And live for Him completely,
> After all He's done for me.

I didn't know it then, but I was singing the secret of life.

I knew the "He" was Jesus, and I knew what He'd "done" was to die for my sins and release me to life here and life hereafter.

And I knew He deserved everything in return.

What I didn't know was how many lessons it takes in life, especially in as basic an area as life's money matters, to find your way to the real freedom which releases His fullness in *all* of life.

In trying to share some of these lessons, I sincerely hope you've been helped by hearing of my stumblings, fumblings and grumblings, as well as by discovering that even someone as equally human as I suppose you are *can* begin to lay hold of a key — the Key to *Everything*.

If it turns out that my lessons from life, along with the wisdom of God's Word, help, I'm going to ask you to give *me* a gift. It's easy to do, and I think you'll enjoy doing it.

I'd like you to sing a second song with me.

A few years ago I was humming a melody I'd learned in

my childhood — an old Welsh tune which nearly every schoolchild has heard at one time or another. Whatever the original title, most of us learned it as "All Through the Night."

As I was driving home on the Los Angeles freeway system one night, I thought as I hummed that song, "That would make a great hymn tune; maybe I should write some lyrics to it sometime."

Weeks went by, and Easter was drawing near. We were approaching what is always a high day on our church calendar: Good Friday. On that day a most unusual spirit seems to always attend our congregation's gathering. Huge crowds come, even before Easter Day, because something has progressively gripped our understanding: The *life* Easter offers is because of the *death* Good Friday commemorates.

Elsewhere and at other times, I've shared with many what I do to resensitize my heart each holy week. Multitudes observe Lent as a pre-Easter discipline, and it's a worthy practice. We need to do *something* to remember that *everything* was given to us at this time — long ago. But while I don't observe the Lenten tradition, I do usually assign a few days to personal, pre-Good-Friday fasting.

I always conclude my fast the same way.

About two hours before the first of our series of Good Friday observances celebrated at The Church On The Way (that first one is at high noon), I go to my private office and serve myself communion. I take a large piece of bread and a large glass of grape juice, and for an extended period of time, I quiet my heart — worshipping, singing, sometimes weeping — and thank Jesus for *everything*.

Two years ago as I was observing this private, tender ritual, the Holy Spirit brought lyrics alive in my mind — lyrics to set to the tune I had hummed and thought would make a hymn.

Those lyrics are here, given as a gift for *your* use, with my request that you'll give *me* the gift of allowing my hymn to become your song. Often. Here it is.

HAIL TO THE CROSS

Come with me to Calv'ry's mountain;
  Come to the Cross.
Come and wash in Calv'ry's fountain;
  Come to the Cross.
    To the place where Christ died for us,
    Where He paid the "Blood-price" for us,
    Come and lift this joyous chorus;
  Come to the Cross.

Praise the Lamb who bled and died there,
  There at the Cross.
Jesus who was crucified there,
  There at the Cross.
    Through His Blood, that crimson token,
    All hell's power has been broken;
    "It is finished" has been spoken,
  There at the Cross.

Here is reason for rejoicing,
  Here at the Cross.
Grounds for highest praises voicing,
  Here at the Cross.
    Here the sin-curse Jesus severed;
    Here He bought us life forever;
    Here He'll keep and leave us never,
  Here at the Cross.

Here is heav'n's eternal treasure;
  God planned the Cross.
Wealth of love in endless measure;
  God planned the Cross.
    Since His Son has bled and died there,
    All my hope for life is tied there,
    For God says I'm justified there;
  God planned the Cross

Jesus saves and Jesus heals us,
　All through the Cross.
By redemption's pow'r He seals us,
　All through the Cross.
　　In the wake of human sinning,
　　Jesus brought a new beginning;
　　By His death this promise winning,
　All through the Cross.

By the Cross we are forgiven;
　Hail to the Cross.
By the Cross we'll enter heaven;
　Hail to the Cross.
　　Through God's love and grace amazing,
　　We shall join in endless praising;
　　So this anthem now we're raising:
　Hail to the Cross!

Copyright © JWH-Annamarie Music

Thank you for reading, and, I hope, for singing those lines. You'll find the melody in the back of the book. You can sing it easily, even if you've never heard it before. It was written for children, and those of us committed to remaining child-like before our Father can always sing those songs.

So let me leave you with that. A book and a song. A book about the Key to Everything and a song about where the Key is found.

It's at the cross.

And knowing Jesus' *giving*, and letting Him teach us how to give like He does, is to find all there is to life.

Everything.

RECEIVING JESUS CHRIST AS LORD AND SAVIOR

IF, AS an earnest reader of this book, you have come to realize your need for a relationship with God through His Son, you can now receive Jesus Christ as your personal Savior. Allow me to help you personally welcome the Lord Jesus into your heart, to be your Savior and to lead you in the matters of your life now and into eternal life forever.

There is no need to delay because an honest heart can approach the loving Father God at any time. So I'd like to invite you to come with me, and let's pray to Him right now.

If it's possible where you are, bow your head or even kneel if you can. In either case, let me pray a simple prayer first. I've added words for you to pray yourself after I have prayed.

My Prayer

Father God, I have the privilege of joining with this child of Yours who is reading this book right now. Thank You for the openness of heart being shown toward You, and praise You for Your promise which says that when we call to You, You will answer.

I know that genuine sincerity is present in this heart which is ready to speak this prayer. So we come to You in the name and through the cross of Your Son, the Lord Jesus. Thank You for hearing.

(Now speak your prayer.)

Your Prayer

Dear God, I am doing this because I believe in Your love for me, and I want to ask You to come to me as I come to You. Please help me now.

First, I thank You for sending Your Son, Jesus, to earth to live and to die for me on the cross. I thank You for the gift of forgiveness of sin that You offer me now, and I pray for that forgiveness.

Forgive me and cleanse my life in Your sight through the blood of Jesus Christ. I am sorry for anything and everything I have ever done that is unworthy in Your sight. Please take away all guilt and shame as I accept the fact that Jesus died to pay for all my sins. Through Him I am now given forgiveness on this earth and eternal life in heaven.

I ask You, Lord Jesus, to please come into my life now. Because You rose from the dead, I know You're alive, and I want You to live with me — now and forever.

I am turning my life over to You and turning from my way to Yours. I invite Your Holy Spirit to fill me and lead me forward in a life that will please the heavenly Father.

Thank You for hearing me. From this day forward, I commit myself to Jesus Christ, Your Son. In His name, amen.

HAIL TO THE CROSS

"All Through the Night"

Trad. Welsh Melody
Words by Jack W. Hayford

1. Come with me to Cal- v'ry's moun - tain, Come to the Cross.

Come and wash in Cal- v'ry's foun - tain, Come to the Cross.

To the place where Christ died for us, Where He paid the "Blood - price" for us,

Come and lift this joy - ous cho- rus, Come to the Cross.

ABOUT THE AUTHOR

Jack Hayford is the well-known pastor of The Church On The Way in Van Nuys, California, America's largest Foursquare church.

He has written more than four hundred musical works and sixteen books, produces a daily radio program and a weekly television program and serves as the senior editorial advisor for Ministsries Today.

He and his wife, Anna, have four children and eight grandchildren.

If you enjoyed *The Key to Everything*,
you'll love these other new Creation House titles:

Primary Purpose
by Ted Haggard

Colorado Springs pastor Ted Haggard shows how charismatic and
evangelical churches in his community have united together in prayer
and spiritual warfare to bring revival and citywide church growth.
This landmark book, foreworded by C. Peter Wagner, is endorsed by
a host of pastors and leaders including John Dawson, Cindy Jacobs,
Jack Hayford, Myles Munroe and Loren Cunningham.

There's a Miracle in Your House
by Tommy Barnett

God wants to do something fantastic with what you already have!
This upbeat, motivating book will revolutionize the way you think
about "impossible" situations and "overwhelming" opportunities.
When God shows you the miracle in the house, you won't
have to look anywhere else.

As for Me and My House
by Dolores Hayford

How many times have you started family devotions, only to get
one more "black mark" on your guilt chart? This simple, fun
devotional guide — based on the Ten Commandments — will help
parents develop quality devotions with their children that will
last not just for a while, but for a lifetime. Endorsed by the
author's son, Jack Hayford.

Available at your local
Christian bookstore or from:

Creation House
600 Rinehart Road
Lake Mary, FL 32746
1-800-283-8494